MY SIDEWALKS ON
SCOTT FORESMAN
READING STREET

W9-AAU-899

Puzzles and Mysteries

Program Authors

Connie Juel, Ph.D.

Jeanne R. Paratore, Ed.D.

Deborah Simmons, Ph.D.

Sharon Vaughn, Ph.D.

Copyright © 2011 by Pearson Education, Inc., or its affiliates. All Rights Reserved. Printed in the United States of America. This publication is protected by copyright, and permission should be obtained from the publisher prior to any prohibited reproduction, storage in a retrieval system, or transmission in any form or by any means, electronic, mechanical, photocopying, recording, or likewise. For information regarding permissions, write to Pearson Curriculum Group Rights & Permissions, One Lake Street, Upper Saddle River, New Jersey 07458.

Pearson, Scott Foresman, and Pearson Scott Foresman are trademarks, in the U.S. and/or other countries, of Pearson Education, Inc., or its affiliates.

PEARSON
Scott Foresman

Glenview, Illinois
Boston, Massachusetts
Chandler, Arizona
Upper Saddle River, New Jersey

ISBN-13: 978-0-328-45289-7
ISBN-10:   0-328-45289-0

10 V011 14

CC1

UNIT 4 Contents

Puzzles and Mysteries

Perception

Contents

Perception

Words 2 the Wise

Perception is all about how we see things. This week you'll explore different ways of seeing things. As you read, think about what you know about perception.

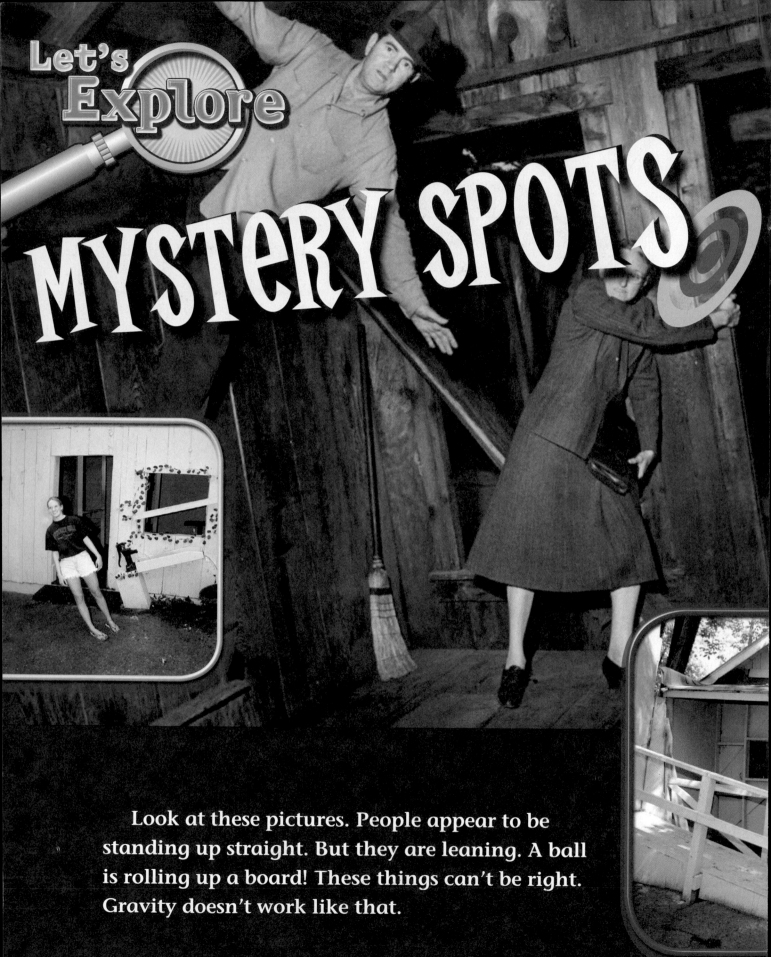

Let's Explore

MYSTERY SPOTS

Look at these pictures. People appear to be standing up straight. But they are leaning. A ball is rolling up a board! These things can't be right. Gravity doesn't work like that.

These are just some of the strange things that occur at Mystery Spots. Mystery Spots are located across the United States. These are places where your perception is turned upside down.

Is there something in the air or ground that causes these weird things to happen? Or is it a trick of your eyes? As one tourist said, "You have to see it to believe it."

HARRY HOUDINI ESCAPES

by Patricia Wydell

IT'S NOT THE TRICK. IT'S THE MAGICIAN. —*Harry Houdini*

Harry Houdini was a great magician. He became famous around the world. Handcuffs and prison cells could not hold him. He escaped from locked boxes full of water. He could make an elephant disappear.

How did he do it? Some of it was hard work and skill. But Houdini was also good at fooling people. Did the elephant really vanish? No, it was an illusion.

Harry Houdini could escape from handcuffs and chains.

Houdini created illusions. An illusion is something that seems to happen but really can't. If a rabbit appeared in an empty hat, it was an illusion because rabbits can't appear out of thin air. And how about the disappearing elephant? You guessed it. It was an illusion. Houdini's tricks fooled people. They thought they saw an elephant vanish, but it didn't really happen.

Houdini being lowered into a box from which he would soon escape

At first, Houdini's act did not impress people. He was a small man. His voice was high, his clothes were old and dirty, and his grammar was poor.

But over the years, Houdini worked to make his act better. He wrote out what he would say. He corrected his grammar. He did exercises to make his hands and feet fast and flexible. To strengthen his lungs, he held his breath in tubs full of water.

Houdini amazes the crowd as he hangs upside down.

Harry Houdini, Master Magician

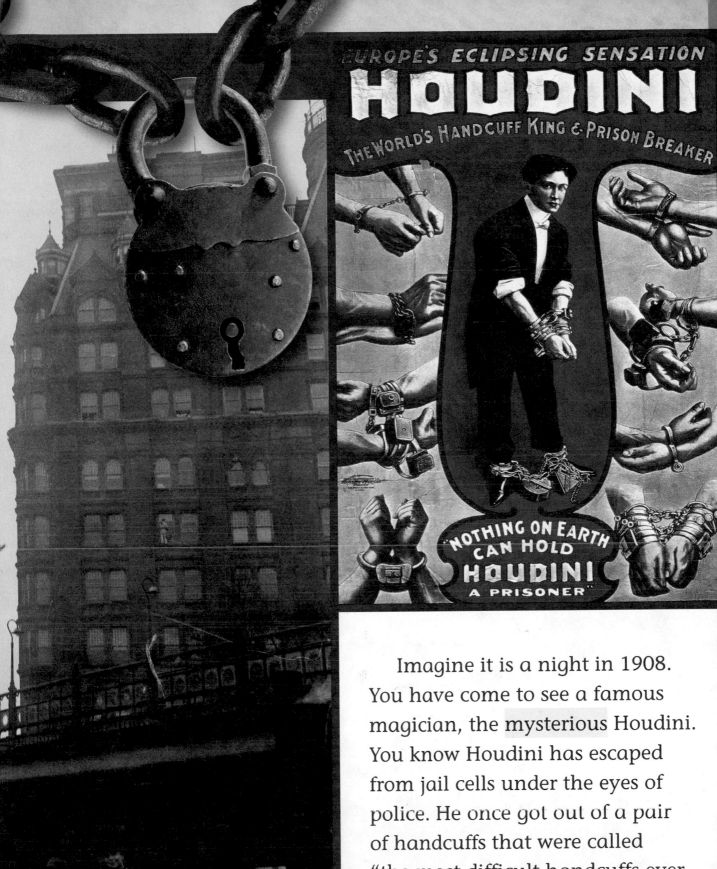

EUROPE'S ECLIPSING SENSATION
HOUDINI
THE WORLD'S HANDCUFF KING & PRISON BREAKER

"NOTHING ON EARTH CAN HOLD HOUDINI A PRISONER"

Imagine it is a night in 1908. You have come to see a famous magician, the mysterious Houdini. You know Houdini has escaped from jail cells under the eyes of police. He once got out of a pair of handcuffs that were called "the most difficult handcuffs ever invented." What will Houdini do tonight?

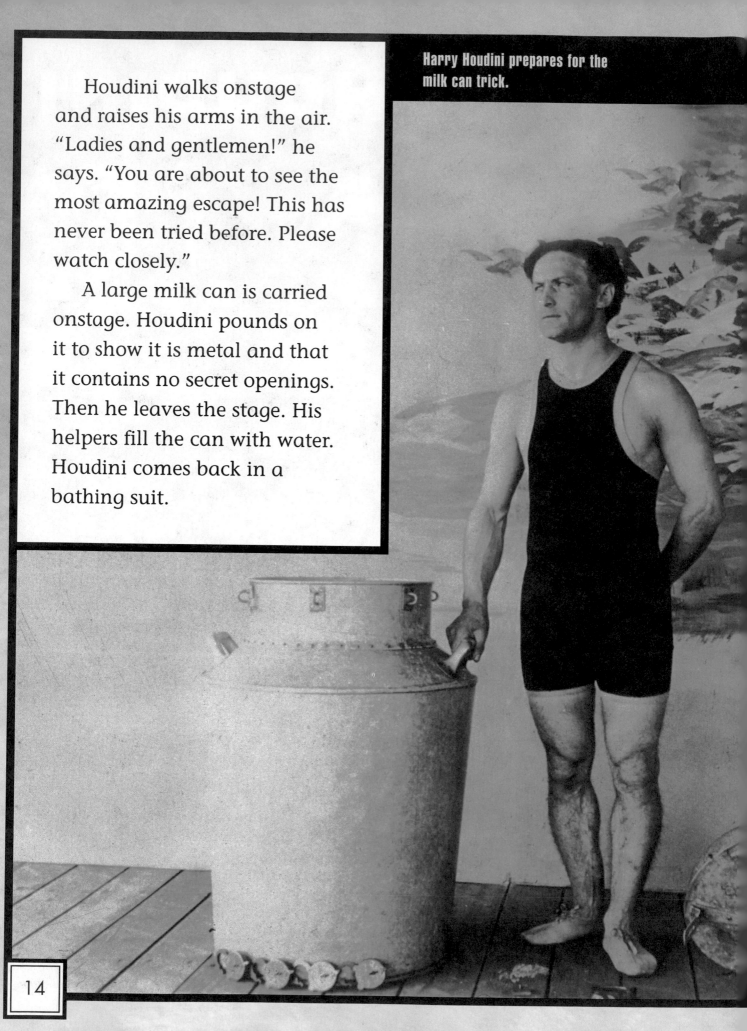

Houdini walks onstage and raises his arms in the air. "Ladies and gentlemen!" he says. "You are about to see the most amazing escape! This has never been tried before. Please watch closely."

A large milk can is carried onstage. Houdini pounds on it to show it is metal and that it contains no secret openings. Then he leaves the stage. His helpers fill the can with water. Houdini comes back in a bathing suit.

Harry Houdini prepares for the milk can trick.

"Ladies and gentlemen," he says, "I am going to climb into this can filled with water."

Houdini is handcuffed. He squeezes into the milk can. The can is locked tight.

If something goes wrong, a helper will break open the can with an ax.

A curtain is placed in front of the can. People look at their watches. Nothing is heard or seen for two minutes. How long can he hold his breath underwater?

Policemen made sure Houdini's handcuffs were secure before locking him in the milk can.

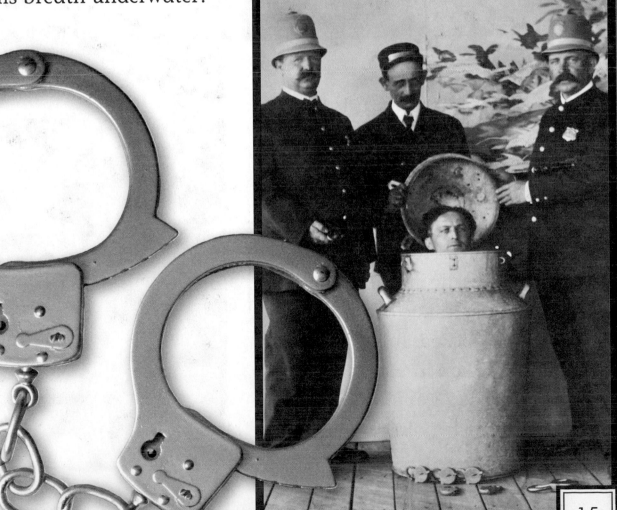

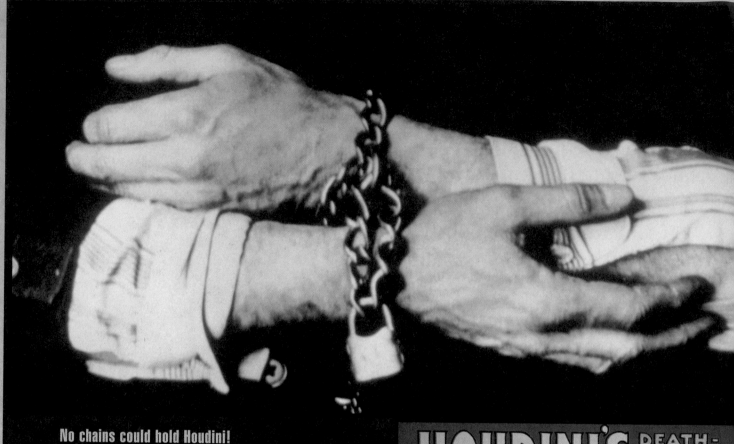

No chains could hold Houdini!

What is happening? Is Houdini dead? People begin to look at the helper with the ax. Is it time to smash open the milk can?

Suddenly, Houdini appears, panting and dripping wet. He looks tired. The curtain is moved. There is the milk can with the cover still locked. It is amazing! How did he do it? Houdini, of course, will not explain. He wants his tricks to remain mysterious.

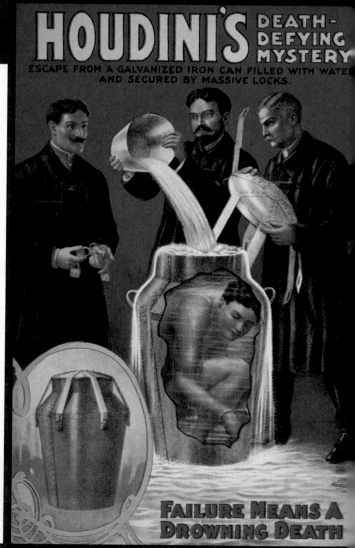

HOUDINI'S DEATH-DEFYING MYSTERY

ESCAPE FROM A GALVANIZED IRON CAN FILLED WITH WATER AND SECURED BY MASSIVE LOCKS.

FAILURE MEANS A DROWNING DEATH

The milk can's cover was locked, but the top part of the can was not really attached to the rest. First, Houdini would push the top off. Next, he would climb out, and then place the top back on. He would stand behind the curtain a few minutes. He would wait until everyone was sure he had drowned. Finally, he would appear. His puffing and panting was an act. Ladies and gentlemen, don't always believe what you see!

WHAT DO *You* THINK?

How did Harry Houdini perform the milk can trick?

STEP 1

STEP 2

STEP 3

Inside a Top Hat

by Karla Kate
illustrated by Franklin Hammond

Hello, I am Puff, a white rabbit that will be pulled from a magician's top hat. I am sitting in a secret box attached underneath a table. I am invisible to the audience.

Above me is a silk top hat. It rests on the table, upside down, covering a hole in the table. The audience can't see that the hole connects to my box. The hat and I are part of an illusion to be performed by the magician.

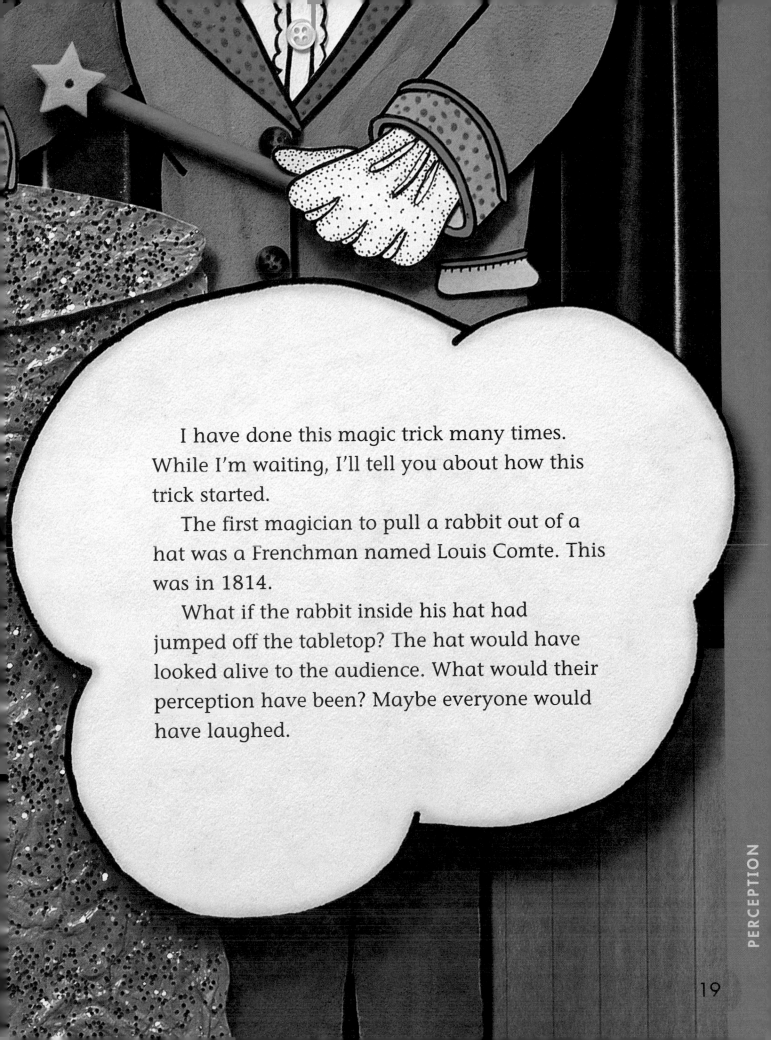

I have done this magic trick many times. While I'm waiting, I'll tell you about how this trick started.

The first magician to pull a rabbit out of a hat was a Frenchman named Louis Comte. This was in 1814.

What if the rabbit inside his hat had jumped off the tabletop? The hat would have looked alive to the audience. What would their perception have been? Maybe everyone would have laughed.

It is almost two hundred years later. Thousands of rabbits have been pulled out of hats. These are the kinds of things I think of as I wait.

Soon the magic show will begin. People in the audience were whispering. Now they are quiet. They wait for the show to begin. I can almost hear their breathing. The lights go down. I imagine many pairs of wide and wondering eyes.

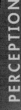

A drum roll starts the show. It's the signal that Marva will soon be onstage. The drum roll fades away. A voice calls out, "Ladies and gentlemen! Please welcome the one . . . the only . . . Marva the Mysterious!"

Now the audience comes to life. Their clapping comes in waves. They applaud for their favorite magician. Their cheers and whistles fill the air. Marva appears onstage.

When the cheering quiets down, I hear Marva step toward the table. I hear a drum roll once again.

Marva removes the hat from the table. I am no longer in the dark. I wait patiently in the box. I hear Marva tell the audience, "As you can see, what I have here is a typical top hat. There is nothing inside. It's just a plain old hat."

Next, Marva returns the hat to the table. "Watch closely!" she announces.

The audience thinks the top hat is not unusual. Their perception is wrong. They don't know that there is a false bottom that Marva will open in order to reach me. They don't know that I am in a secret box, getting ready to surprise them and show them that their eyes have deceived them.

The drum roll continues. It grows louder as one of Marva's expert hands reaches in and secretly opens the bottom of the hat. The next thing I know, she pulls me out of the box, through the hat, and into the lights. She holds me up in the air for all to see. I am no longer invisible.

The audience is amazed. A young child in the front row turns to his mother. He asks, "How did she do that? How did she make that white bunny come out of the hat?"

My work is over. Marva's show has barely started, and I am already finished. In a few seconds, a helper will take me behind the curtain. I can't wait to do this again tomorrow night!

What Do You Think?

How does Marva the Mysterious prepare for her trick?

DISAPPEARING ACT!

THIS TRICK IS EASY TO DO. The secret is to make the audience look where you want them to look. Read these steps and try the trick.

1 Hold a quarter out in your hand. Point to the quarter with a pencil. Say: "Ladies and gentlemen, I will now make a quarter disappear. Please watch carefully. Do you see the date on this quarter?"

2 Tap the quarter with the pencil. Bring the pencil up high, next to your head. Tap the quarter again. Count as you tap. Look only at the quarter. Say: *"One. Two."*

3 The third time you raise the pencil, tuck it behind your ear. Then bring your empty hand down to the quarter. Keep your eyes on the quarter. Say: *"Three. Oh, no, look what I did! I made the PENCIL disappear! I'm sorry, folks. I goofed."*

4 Turn your body to the side so everyone can see your ear. Point to the pencil. Say: *"Just a joke, folks. I stuck it behind my ear."*

5 While pointing to the pencil, quickly drop the quarter into your pocket. Then put your hand out again, this time closed in a fist.

6 Point to your fist with the pencil. (Everyone thinks the quarter is still in your hand.) Tap your fist with the pencil. Say: *"I promised to make a quarter vanish. So let's get to it. One. Two. Three. Presto!"*

7 **OPEN YOUR FIST. THE QUARTER HAS DISAPPEARED!**

Word Play

How many words can you make from the letters in the word *mysterious*? Find 5–10 words that each contains three or more letters. Then, with a friend, take turns using the words in sentences.

MYSTERIOUS

Making Connections

What illusions did Houdini and Marva create for their audiences?

On Paper

Houdini wore a bathing suit when he performed the milk can trick. Marva wore a tuxedo when she performed the rabbit trick. You're a magician! What would *you* wear?

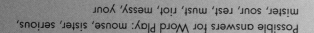

Possible answers for Word Play: mouse, sister, serious, mister, sour, rest, must, riot, messy, your

30

Contents

WILD THINGS

Words 2 the Wise

Animals and people behave in different ways. Or do they? What do you know about **animal behavior**? Think about it as you read.

Amazing

Beaver lodges look like piles of sticks. Notice that the edges of the pile are underwater so the beavers can enter without predators seeing them.

Beavers are amazing builders. Their homes are called lodges. They are built on the water. They are made from sticks and branches. Beavers pack the outside with mud. In the winter the mud hardens like cement. This helps protect them from predators and bad weather.

Beavers swim underwater to enter their lodges. Inside it is dark. They make holes in the roof to let out steam. Beavers will usually live in their homes for only a year.

Homes

Hermit crabs also have amazing homes. But they do not build their own homes. They use empty snail shells. The hermit crab has a soft stomach. This lets it squeeze into the shell. The crab carries its portable home on its back.

Anemones act as alarm systems for hermit crabs. Anemones attach themselves to the shell. They protect the hermit crab from its enemy, the octopus. A hermit crab's home is safer with anemones attached to the shell.

The hermit crab drags its bulky home across the ocean floor. At the first sign of trouble, it hides inside its shell.

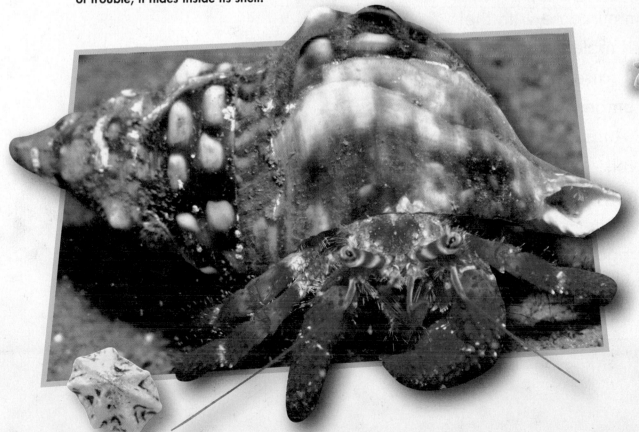

Keeping Baby Safe

by Penelope C. Price

Sharing the Responsibility

Humans and animals have a lot in common. Both protect and care for their young. Both also communicate with their young. Both male and female animals help raise their young.

Emperor penguins live in the Antarctic. A mother penguin travels up to sixty miles to lay a single egg. Then she gives it to the father penguin. He protects the egg for two to three months until it hatches.

He balances the egg on the tops of his webbed feet. He keeps it warm in a pouch. The father does not eat while waiting for the egg to hatch. He may lose half of his body weight.

The mother penguin returns soon after the egg hatches. She carries chewed fish in her crop. The crop is a place in her throat where she can carry food for her chick. The penguin parents work together.

Knowing Mom and Dad

Sometimes young children wander away from their parents. Children then become frightened. They need their parents to be close. Children and animals act afraid out of instinct.

Baby swans are called cygnets. (SIG-nits) The adult swans take the cygnets to a pond. This is where they catch their first meal. Cygnets can walk and swim right after they are born. A cygnet always recognizes its own parents. Instinct tells the cygnet to follow its mother everywhere.

Going for a Ride

Humans can take their children by their arms or by the hand. But how do most animals carry their young?

Lion cubs cannot walk for three weeks after they are born. The mother lion must gently grab the loose skin on her cub's back. She carries it with her teeth. The cub stops wiggling when it is lifted. That makes it easier for the mother to carry it.

wah!

purr.

Keeping in Touch

What happens if your little sister cries? Your mom or dad might talk quietly to her. They tell her that she is safe. The sounds of their voices comfort her.

Communication between animals and their babies is like this. Young raccoons make high-pitched noises when they think they are alone. They sound like a human baby crying. Mother raccoons answer with soft purring sounds. This calms the babies. It lets them know they are safe.

Sensing Trouble

Human and animal parents sense when their young ones are in danger.

Animals make different sounds to warn young ones. The mute swan communicates by making a barking sound to her cygnets.

The wallaby is similar to a kangaroo. A baby wallaby is called a joey. A mother wallaby thumps the ground with her feet if she senses danger. The joey hears the thumping. It runs back to her and climbs into her pouch.

On Their Own

Most human parents will care for their children a long time. The time period is much shorter for many animals. Bears take care of their cubs until they are about seventeen months old. Then the mother forces the young out of her territory.

For young clownfish the time period is much shorter. The female clownfish lays hundreds of eggs on a flat rock. Then she leaves. The male watches over the eggs until they hatch. He fans the eggs with his fins. He also eats eggs that have been damaged.

The young fish that hatch from the eggs are called fry. They are left alone once the eggs hatch. Clownfish are born knowing everything they need to know to survive. They are ready to go off on their own.

What do you think?

Which two creatures care for their young in a similar way?

Black Feather
and the Ravens

by Robert Kausal
illustrated by Richard Downs

A Native American legend from the Anishinabe [ah-NISH-i-nah-beh] people of North America

Black Feather was a man who liked to be with ravens. The people in his village thought he was odd. They would often laugh at him. He would sit high up in the tallest trees, watching these clever black birds. Black Feather loved the way that ravens flew. He liked watching them play. He spoke to them with his own caw, caw response.

One day a raven flew to the branch where Black Feather sat. "Why do you watch us?" the raven asked.

Black Feather jumped. "I didn't mean to upset you," said Black Feather. "But I am amazed by you and your friends. I only wish to learn more about you."

"As long as you do not hurt us," the raven said, "it would be an honor to have you live with us and learn our language."

For many months the ravens taught Black Feather about how they lived and communicated. He saw the kinds of relationships they had with other animals. He learned how they outsmart eagles and coyotes. Soon the ravens accepted Black Feather as a friend. They treated him as they did each other.

One day a raven dropped a walnut on top of Black Feather's head. "Ouch!" said Black Feather. He rubbed his head where the walnut hit him.

Many of the ravens laughed so hard they almost fell out of the trees. "Why is everyone picking on me?" Black Feather asked the raven.

The raven looked surprised. "We are not making fun of you," he said. "This is how we play."

Soon, Black Feather started playing jokes on them. He would scare them by howling like a coyote. He would climb high up in the trees and fill their nests with walnuts. These tricks made him even more popular.

One day a raven swooped down and pecked him very hard on the head. Then another raven swooped down and pecked him on the head. They were also calling him mean names.

This is not funny, thought Black Feather. He questioned his relationship with the ravens. He decided to return to his village.

Black Feather told his people how smart ravens are. He told them about the tricks they like to play on each other.

Black Feather was telling the children a story when he heard a caw coming from a tree. It was a raven.

"Black Feather," the raven said, "you are closer to us than any human has ever been. Why did you leave?"

"I don't understand why the ravens were so mean," Black Feather said. "They called me names."

"We said those things because we think of you as one of us," the raven said.

Black Feather stood quietly thinking. Then he gave his response. "There is so much I don't understand about ravens. Maybe we are too different."

The raven said, "It is your choice, Black Feather. Do you want to quit or learn more about us?"

"What's the use?" Black Feather said. "I can't even fly!"

Suddenly, laughter shook the trees. Black Feather knew that other ravens were listening.

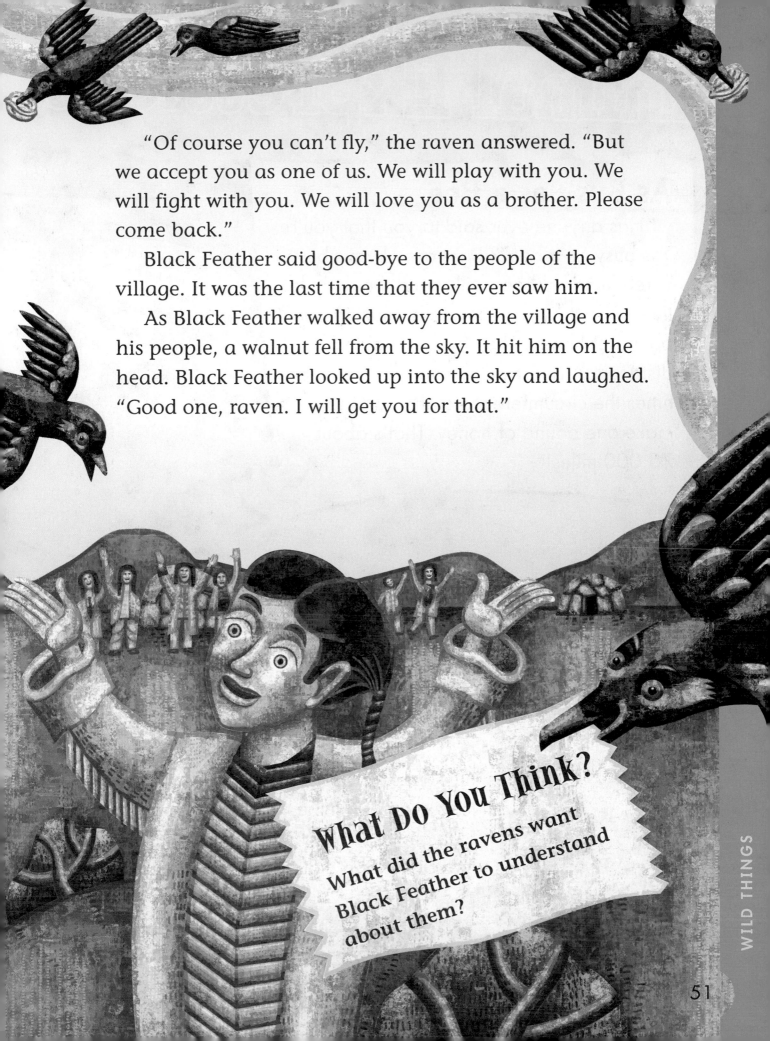

"Of course you can't fly," the raven answered. "But we accept you as one of us. We will play with you. We will fight with you. We will love you as a brother. Please come back."

Black Feather said good-bye to the people of the village. It was the last time that they ever saw him.

As Black Feather walked away from the village and his people, a walnut fell from the sky. It hit him on the head. Black Feather looked up into the sky and laughed. "Good one, raven. I will get you for that."

What Do You Think?
What did the ravens want Black Feather to understand about them?

Animal Expressions

As Busy as a Bee

Has anyone ever said to you that you're "as busy as a bee"? Bees are always busy. Three hundred bees will spend their whole lives, about five or six weeks, making one pound of honey. They fly an amazing distance. A bee would have to travel three times the circumference of the Earth to make one pound of honey. That's about 75,000 miles!

circumference: distance around a sphere like the Earth

Watch Like a Hawk

"I have to watch my little brother like a hawk." Why a hawk instead of a robin or a sparrow? A hawk's eyesight is eight times more powerful than a human's. Hawks can sit in the very top of trees or fly high above a meadow and see the slightest movement of a mouse in the grass below.

"I've got to keep working. He's watching me!"

Hungry as a Horse

Have you heard someone say, "I'm as hungry as a horse"? Some horses don't know when to stop eating. If a horse is let out into a rich pasture where grain is growing or if it finds a large bag of dry oats or other grain, it may eat until it gets sick.

"When will he ever stop eating!"

"That's my boy!"

The Lion's Share

"You get the lion's share of the cake." Is that good? Yes, because the lion gets the most. When the pride of lions and lionesses catch a prey, they eat in a certain order. The male lion eats first, and then the lionesses take their share.

As the Crow Flies

When asking for directions, you might hear someone answer, "It takes about an hour as the crow flies." The fastest way to get somewhere is to walk straight towards your destination. Unfortunately, we can't always do this. Things get in the way. When a crow flies somewhere, it can fly straight to its destination.

"I don't need to zig-zag. I'll go straight there!"

"Hey, that's not fair!"

"I can see everything from here!"

A Bird's-Eye View

A "bird's-eye view" of the situation means you can see it all. From high above a bird can see everything below. Sometimes we need to see more than what is in front or in back of us. That's when you want a bird's-eye view. A bird's-eye view helps us come up with the best solution.

"Don't try this at home kids!"

Take the Bull by the Horns

During a difficult situation you might hear someone say, "You need to take the bull by the horns." The horns are a bull's most dangerous part. When you take the bull by the horns you are taking control of a situation. You are also taking action and facing a problem directly.

The Early Bird Catches the Worm

This year's new video game is selling fast. Your dad wakes you up at six in the morning and says, "The early bird gets the worm!" What he means is that you have to get up early if you want to get what you want. If you are slow, others might get to the store before you and the game will be sold out.

Zzzz

EEK!

"He's all mine!"

55

4 YOU 2 Do

Word Play

How many words can you make from these words? Rearrange the letters to make 2 to 5 words from each word.

relationships

instinct

communication

Making Connections

Why is it important to understand animals?

On Paper

Create your own folk tale. Tell a story about an animal who teaches someone a lesson.

Possible answers for Word Play: ship, shape, real, relation, noise, hip; in, tin; cat, nation, commit

Contents

SECRET CODES

Let's Explore

Words 2 the Wise

Got a secret? Want to keep it secret but share it with a pal? Then **secret codes** are for you! Read to find out about different kinds of secret codes.

Sports

A batter steps up to the plate. The batter looks at the coach. The coach holds up some fingers. Then he rubs his head and points to his eye. He touches his nose. The batter and coach exchange looks. The batter interprets the signals and nods.

On the next pitch, the runner on first base takes off for second at full speed. The batter swings and hits a ground ball into right field. Everyone is safe!

Signals

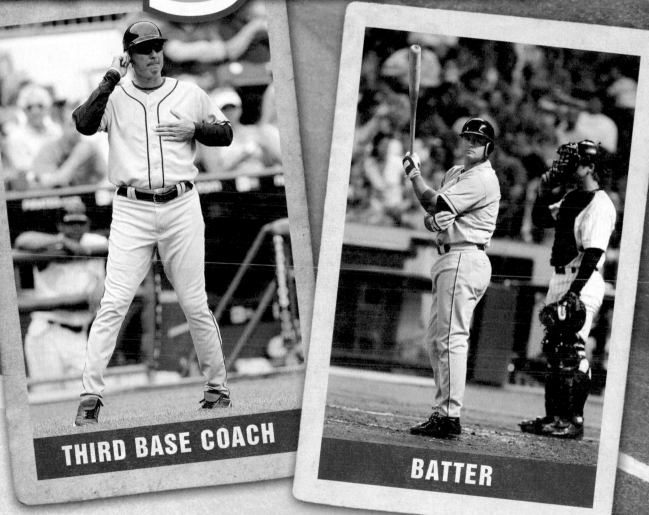

THIRD BASE COACH

BATTER

What is going on? The coach has sent the batter visible signals. He used a secret code to call a hit-and-run play. He told the batter where to hit the ball. He also sent a message to the runner on first base. He told the runner to take off for second base on the next pitch.

61

Other sports use secret codes too. In football the quarterback calls plays using a code. These codes can be very creative. The quarterback might say, "twins right, scram left, 585, crab." This tells the players where to line up, how to block, and where to run to catch the ball. It tells the whole team when to start the play.

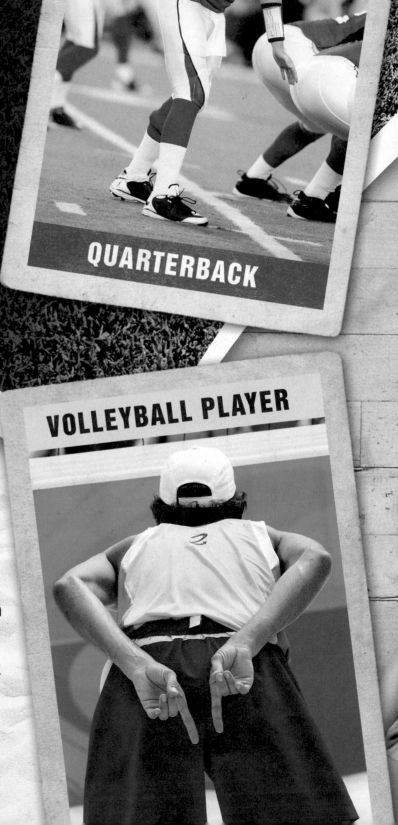

QUARTERBACK

VOLLEYBALL PLAYER

Have you ever seen a doubles volleyball game? Players transmit messages to their partners with hand signals behind their backs. This conceals the signals from the other team. Two fingers down can mean, "I will block the ball at an angle."

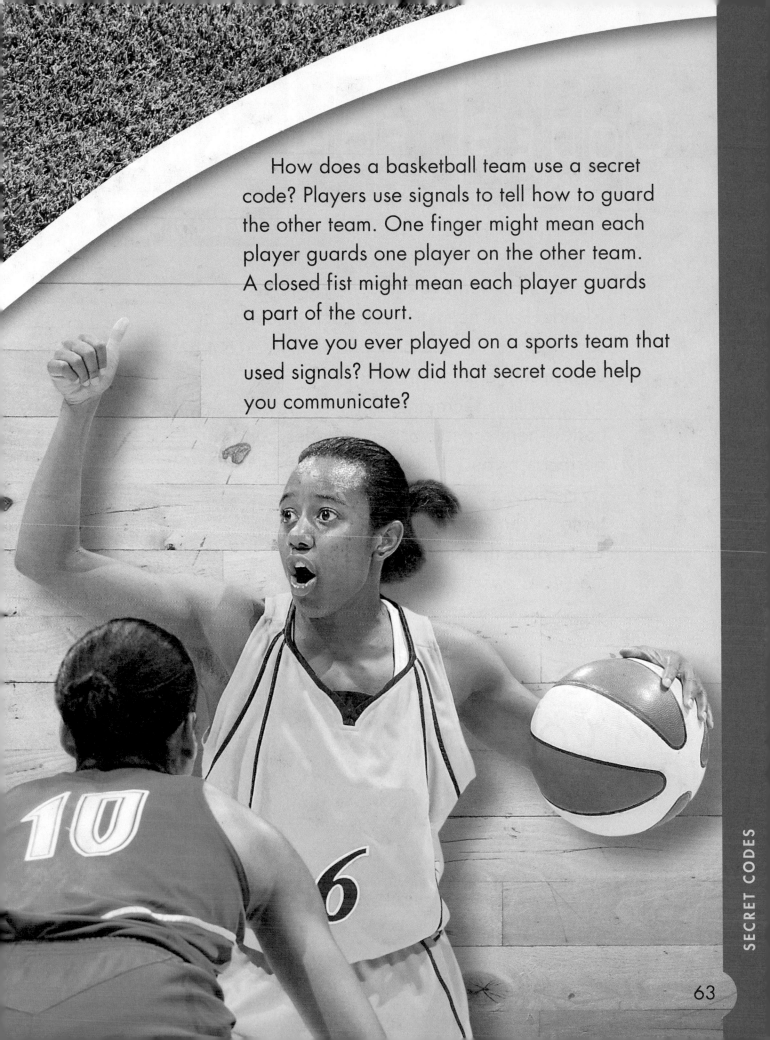

How does a basketball team use a secret code? Players use signals to tell how to guard the other team. One finger might mean each player guards one player on the other team. A closed fist might mean each player guards a part of the court.

Have you ever played on a sports team that used signals? How did that secret code help you communicate?

CODES FOR KIDS

by Jeff Putnam

You want to have a meeting with your friends. But it needs to be a secret meeting in a secret place. There's only one way to arrange it—transmit a secret message!

To write a secret message, you need a secret code. There are lots of secret codes. One is perfect for you.

Here is one of the easiest codes: write all the words backward. What does this secret message say?

!YAROOH
ERA UOY
!RENNIW EHT

Message: Hooray! You are the winner!

64

JASON CALLED HER. HE FELL OFF HIS BIKE. DID YOU MEET HIS SISTER AT THE SWIMMING POOL? THEY WENT TO THE MOVIE LAST NIGHT.

Another secret code uses a piece of paper called a mask. A mask is simple to make. Start by cutting small windows in a piece of paper. Cut one window for each word or part of a word in your secret message.

Now place your mask over another piece of paper. Write your secret message in the windows. Then remove the mask and write other words around your secret message words. This will conceal them. Your friends will be able to interpret the message by placing the mask over the bottom paper. But no one else will!

CALL OFF MEET ING TO NIGHT.

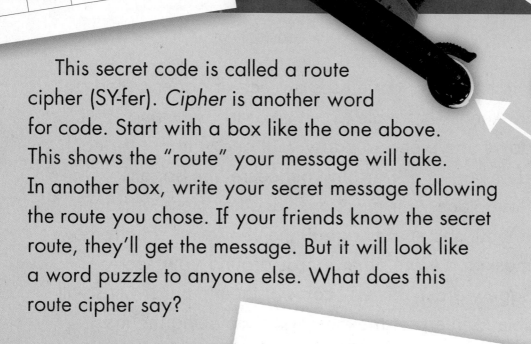

This secret code is called a route cipher (SY-fer). *Cipher* is another word for code. Start with a box like the one above. This shows the "route" your message will take. In another box, write your secret message following the route you chose. If your friends know the secret route, they'll get the message. But it will look like a word puzzle to anyone else. What does this route cipher say?

The route above tells you where this secret message starts.

HE	H	O	L
C	B	T	O	A
R	A	R	K	N
O	C	E	U	I
P	K	D	N	T

Message: Tina, look under the back porch.

MEE W

Another kind of code uses a ruler. Place a ruler on a piece of paper. Print the letters of your message above the inch and half-inch marks on the ruler. Then fill in other letters between your letters. This will conceal your secret message. How will your friends know which letters to read? They can place their own rulers under the message to find the right letters.

MSEQEWTEARTTTKHYEUPIAORPKAASTD4G

Write the letters at the inch and half-inch marks to uncover this secret message.

PARK

Message: Meet at the park at 4.

YLS IPX

A B C D E F G H I J K L M N O P

Z Y X W V U T S R P O N M L K J I H G F E D C B A

Another cool code scrambles letters. No one can read the message without knowing the key. Here's how to make a key. Cut two slits in a strip of paper. Slide a thinner paper strip through the slits. On the first piece of paper, write the letters of the alphabet in order. On the thinner paper strip, write the alphabet backward twice. Be sure to keep the same amount of space between letters on both strips.

Message: Rex has our book.

BVY OBBF.

QRSTUVWXYZ

ZYXWVUTSRQ ONMLKJIHGFEDCBA

Next, choose a key letter. In the message above, the key letter is *P*. The inside strip is placed so that *P* is right under *A* on the back strip. Now read up. *P* stands for *A*. *O* becomes *B*, *N* becomes *C*, and so on. If your friends know the key letter, they can read your secret message. You can change your key letter any time. Just slide a different letter under *A*.

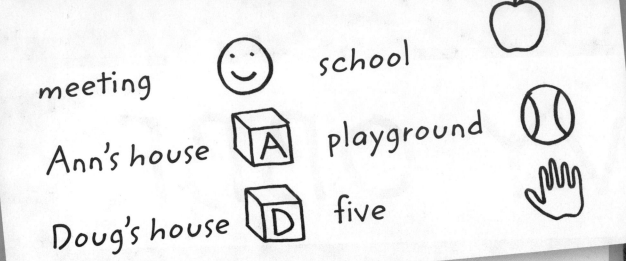

meeting ☺ school 🍎

Ann's house 🅰 playground 🎾

Doug's house 🅳 five ✋

Have you ever seen Chinese writing? Many written Chinese words are simple pictures. These pictures stand for ideas.

You can use the same method to write in secret code. Get creative! A drawing of an apple might mean "school." A drawing of a face might mean "a meeting." A drawing of a hand might mean "five." With your own picture code, you and your friends will be able to exchange top-secret messages.

Where is the meeting? What time is it?

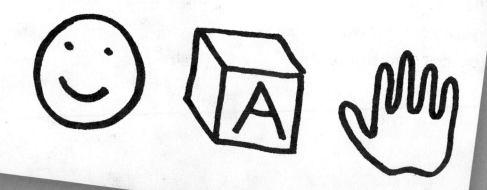

Message: Meeting at Ann's house at 5

This person is sending a Morse code message.

Another way to make sure your message is not visible to others is not to write it at all! Have you heard of Morse code? It exchanges letters and numbers for long and short bits of sound.

Morse code is not a secret code. Many people understand it. But you can make your own code using sounds. Choose noises to represent different letters or words. It won't be quiet, but it will be secret!

WHAT DO YOU THINK?

How is the code that uses a mask like the code that uses a ruler? How are they different?

· A CASE OF ·
CAT AND MOUSE

by Monica Steele • illustrated by Nancy Lane

Donna and Zack studied the piece of paper. It was from Jason. Jason had gone to visit his grandmother, but before he left he sent a message to Donna and Zack. They were all members of the Codemasters Club. They used pictures for words to conceal their messages from nosey people.

"There's a lady and the number 323 inside a house," Zack said.

"That means Mrs. Bittle, who lives at 323 Maple Street," Donna said.

"The next pictures are an eye, a half-moon, and a book," Zack continued.

"I can interpret that," said Donna. "That means he saw her last night and learned something important."

"The last line has a hat and a mouse," Zack added.

Donna gasped and put her hand over her mouth. She exchanged a shocked look with Zack. "I can't believe it," she whispered. "You know what *that* means."

"Mrs. Bittle is a spy!" Zack whispered.
"Is it possible? What should we do?"

"We'll have to watch her," Donna
answered. "If she's a spy, she's very clever—
and maybe even dangerous!"

"She seems like an ordinary neighbor
to me," Zack said.

"I told you she was clever," Donna answered.
"That's what she wants us to think."

"I guess," Zack said. "But I saw her weeding her flower garden yesterday. Do spies have flower gardens?"

"Of course they do," Donna said, "if they're trying to make us think they're regular people. Let's meet after dinner tonight and watch her house."

The two friends met and hid in the bushes by Mrs. Bittle's house. They were barely visible.

"What are we watching for?" whispered Zack.

"Anything strange," Donna whispered back. "She might try to transmit a message to someone. Spies have creative ways of sending messages."

An hour passed. Zack yawned and looked at his watch. "I have to go home," he said.

Just then, Donna pointed to a window. "Look!" she whispered. They watched in silence as the window shade moved up and down, and then up and down again two more times.

"It's a signal!" Zack whispered. "It must be!"

"But what does it mean?" Donna asked. "And who is it for?"

"I don't know," Zack replied. "We'll have to come back tomorrow to watch for more clues."

The next day, Donna and Zack hid in a different part of Mrs. Bittle's yard. Through the open window, they could hear her talking on the telephone.

"OK, then," she said. "Tomorrow night at nine."

"She's going to meet someone," Donna said. "It's probably her spy boss."

"We'll have to follow her," Zack replied.

"I'm glad Jason is getting home tomorrow," Donna said. "He can help us."

The next day, Donna and Zack couldn't wait to talk to
Jason. They told him all about their discoveries.

"Mrs. Bittle's a spy?" Jason asked. He looked confused.
"Who told you that?"

"You did!" cried Donna. "In your message!"

"The last line of your message had a hat and a mouse,"
Zack said. "A mouse means 'spy'."

Jason chuckled. "That wasn't a mouse. That was a
little cat!"

"But a cat means 'school'!" Donna cried.

"Yes," said Jason. "Mrs. Bittle took a job at the middle school. She'll be our teacher next year."

Just then, Mrs. Bittle came out and walked over to the kids. "You'll get to meet my brother soon. I'm going to pick him up at the airport tonight," she said.

"Your brother?" the three friends said together.

"Yes, he's very handy at fixing things," said Mrs. Bittle. "I hope he can fix my window shade. It keeps getting stuck."

Donna, Zack, and Jason looked at each other. What a case of cat and mouse!

WHAT DO YOU THINK?

What did Mrs. Bittle do that made her seem like an ordinary neighbor? What made her seem like a spy?

Leonardo's Secret Code

A Great Inventor

Leonardo da Vinci (lee-oh-NAR-doh dah VIN-chee) was one of the greatest inventors in history. Leonardo lived in Italy five hundred years ago. His notebooks are filled with drawings of inventions. He drew a parachute. He drew an army tank. He even drew a helicopter!

A Secret Code

Leonardo wanted to conceal his ideas from others, so he wrote in secret code. To read it, you had to look at its reflection in a mirror. Leonardo became so used to mirror writing that he wrote most of his notes this way.

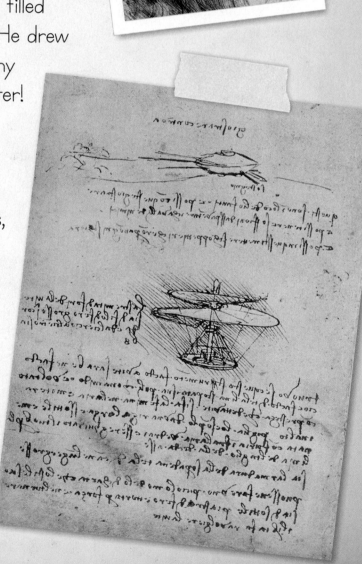

Try the Code!

Do you have an idea that you want to conceal from others? Why not write it in mirror code!

1. Get a sheet of paper and a pencil. Place the pencil on the **right** side of the paper.

2. Write a sentence backward, from right to left. Be sure to reverse each letter. For example, **c** would be **ɔ**.

3. When you are done, try to read your sentence from left to right. It looks like nonsense, doesn't it?

   Now hold your paper in front of a mirror and read it in the mirror. Presto! The **real** sentence appears!

4 you 2 Do

Word Play

These words are written in backward code. Figure out the secret words.

1. t e r p r e t n i
2. l a e c n o c
3. e l b i s i v
4. t i m s n a r t
5. e v i t a e r c
6. e g n a h c x e

Making Connections

Donna and Zack got Jason's secret code mixed up. What might happen if members of a sports team got their signals mixed up during a game?

On Paper

Make up your own code or use one you learned about. Write a secret message to a friend.

Answers for Word Play: 1. interpret, 2. conceal, 3. visible, 4. transmit, 5. creative, 6. exchange

Contents

COMMUNICATION

Words 2 the Wise

We have many ways to **communicate** with each other. As you read, think about how you communicate with other people every day.

Commu

...nication

It's easy to send a message today. We can just pick up the phone. Or we can send an e-mail. But in the past, sending messages took a long time.

Ancient Greeks lit fires on high towers to communicate. American Indians beat drums. Sailors signaled ships with flags. People even tied messages to the legs of carrier pigeons! Each of these forms of communication was limited. You couldn't send your message great distances. And you couldn't say very much.

Telephones, cell phones, and e-mail have replaced the drum and the pigeon. Today, we can send messages across the globe in seconds. Satellites allow people on different continents to talk to each other at the same time! Now, the distance between two points can be closed by a push of a button.

How will we communicate in the future?
with pictures and sound? or how about holograms?
What ways can you imagine to communicate?

Sending the Message

How 100 Years Changed Communication by Daniel Harris

Let's look at how a young girl could have used different ways to send a message 100 years ago.

Communicating in 1900

Imagine it's the year 1900. Sarah and her parents have traveled from New York to California. Sarah decides to write a letter to her grandma in New York. She wants to let her know that her family has arrived.

Dear Grandma,

Our train arrived in California today. The trip from New York took 4 days! California is so different from New York. There is no snow. It is warm here. The sun shines all day.

Love, Sarah

Coded Messages

Sarah's letter will take nearly a week to get to New York by train. But in 1900, there was a faster way. Sarah could have sent a telegram. Her message would have been shorter. Telegram companies charged for each word.

A telegraph operator would send her message in Morse code. Morse code uses dots and dashes for each letter of the alphabet. Sarah's message would have looked like this.

Her message would be decoded in New York, and a messenger would deliver it to Grandma.

From Crank to Ringtone

Why didn't Sarah have a phone conversation with Grandma? In 1900, few people had phones. Phone lines were still being strung across the United States, and phone service was expensive. In those days, phones hung on the wall in wooden boxes.

By 1915, phone lines stretched across the United States. Callers turned a crank to make a call. They needed an operator's help. The first phone service was bad. Conversations were often hard to hear, and calls were sometimes cut off.

Right: An early crank telephone

Far right: A telephone switchboard and operator in the 1940s

COMMUNICATIONS TIME LINE 1900

Before the telephone and telegraph, people communicated by writing letters.

1900
Telegraph machine

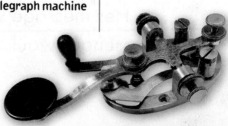

92

Rotary phones like this one required callers to dial each number.

Over the years, phones improved. By the 1920s, people could dial a phone number without an operator's help. In 1956, speakerphones appeared. You didn't have to hold a handset. Then in the 1960s, Touch-Tone phones replaced dial phones.

Today, cell phones are everywhere. Many callers have their own ringtones. They can send instant messages. Cell phones are even used to download music and videos from the Internet. You no longer have to stay at home to receive calls!

Communication has never been easier! You can use your phone to make calls, log on to the Internet, download music, and send pictures and text messages!

1910

1915
First transcontinental telephone call

1920

1920
First commercial radio broadcast

1923
First pictures seen on TV

Birth of the Computer

The first computer was built in the 1940s. It was called the Electronic Numerical Integrator and Computer. It filled a whole room! It weighed nearly as much as an elephant. Early computers could do simple math.

In 1969, four universities had computers "talk" to each other. Each computer became part of a group, or network. This network grew into the Internet. In 1972, computers sent the first person-to-person communication. It was the first electronic mail, or e-mail.

The Electronic Numerical Integrator and Computer (ENIAC) is shown here. It was built at the end of World War II.

1930

1940

1925
Electric radio

1939
First TV broadcast

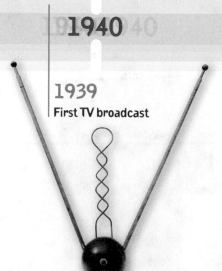

94

Right: An early personal computer
Below: Sperry Univac mainframe computers built in 1964

The first personal computer (PC) was available in 1981. Computers sat on desks instead of filling a room. Later, even smaller laptop computers were sold.

The Internet grew quickly in the 1980s. The World Wide Web started in 1989. It is made up of thousands of Web sites. Internet users can find information easily on the Web. People all over the world shop, bank, and communicate through computers.

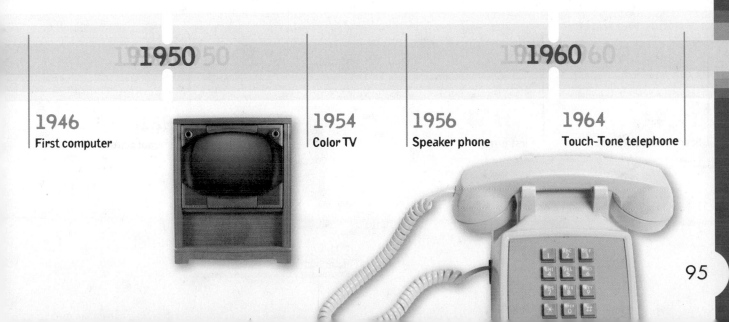

1950 **1960**

1946
First computer

1954
Color TV

1956
Speaker phone

1964
Touch-Tone telephone

Instant Communication

E-mail is everywhere! People send e-mail messages in a kind of code. Here are a few examples of the symbols, or codes, people use.

LOL = laugh out loud   **BTW** = by the way
TU = thank you   **2 B** = to be

You can combine keyboard symbols to make emoticons. Emoticons tell how you feel. Combine keyboard symbols to make these faces.

: -) happy   : - (sad   >: - < mad

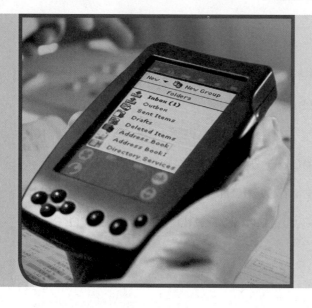

Computers have become small enough to fit into the palm of your hand.

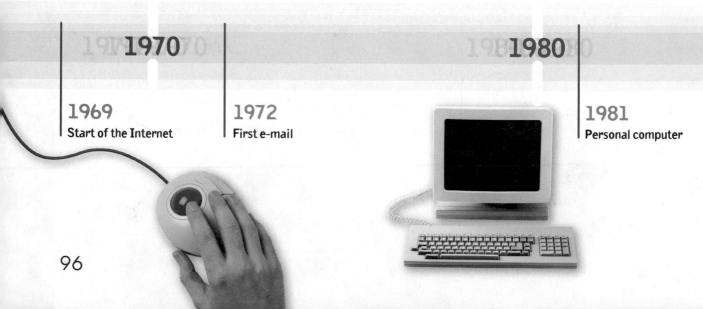

1970

1980

1969
Start of the Internet

1972
First e-mail

1981
Personal computer

Imagine that Sarah was sending a message to her grandmother today. It might look like this:

To: Grandma

Hi! :-) We made it. BTW I forgot my sunscreen! I'm red as a beet! : - (

Grandmother might have replied:

To: Sarah

TU for the message! Glad U R safe. How does it feel 2 B a vegetable? LOL : -)

Back in 1900 Sarah couldn't have dreamed of computers or e-mail. Imagine how we will communicate a hundred years from now.

1990

1989
World Wide Web

What Do You Think?

How has communication changed in 100 years?

Trading Phrases

by Karolyn Kendrick

A Confusing Conversation

Imagine this scene at a local sandwich shop.

"I'll have a hero and a shake."

"Make mine an Italian and a frappe."

"A grinder and a cabinet, please."

The person working there shouts, "Hey, we do not sell furniture! My sandwiches are American, not Italian. And if you want a hero, talk to Superman."

The United States has many regions. In each region residents speak a dialect of English. They use different words and pronunciations for the same thing.

People in New England call a submarine sandwich a "grinder." Or they order a "frappe" (frap). This is a milk shake.

In Rhode Island people call a milk shake a "cabinet." Maybe it is because milk shake mixers came in cabinets, or heavy wooden boxes.

A submarine sandwich is a "hero" in New York. It is a "hoagie" in Philadelphia. And it is a "poor boy" in New Orleans.

Sub sandwiches are "hoagies" in Philadelphia. In New Orleans, the same sandwich is a "poor boy."

Hey, can I have a bite?

hoagie? hero? poor boy?

In Their Own Words

Regional names are part of the history of a place. Sometimes they are a clue to where people came from. For example, many Italian immigrants settled around Maine. In Italy they made big sandwiches. So, in Maine a sub is called an "Italian."

Language experts study dialects. They research local words. They study how local words become popular.

Experts noticed that many people in the Northeast call certain shoes "sneakers." The same shoes are called "tennis shoes" in the Midwest and "gym shoes" around Chicago and Detroit.

What you call "sneakers" may be tennis shoes, gym shoes, or trainers to other kids.

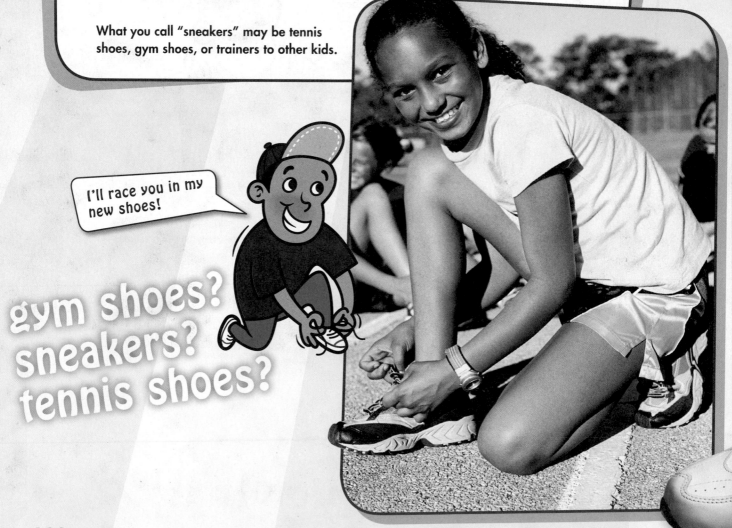

I'll race you in my new shoes!

gym shoes?
sneakers?
tennis shoes?

100

Sometimes a local word appears in different places. Water fountains are a good example. In Milwaukee and Boston water fountains are called "bubblers." Word detectives discovered that the first drinking fountains were called bubblers. Even though they're called drinking fountains today, the name bubbler stuck in some places.

What do you call this machine? It depends on where you live.

Excuse me. Can I have a sip too?

bubblers?
drinking
fountains?

Word Changes

Look at the picture below. Imagine that your friend is standing on a street corner. You are on the corner diagonally across. You might say your friend is "catty-corner" from you if you are from the south. Experts say this phrase is tied to the French language. "Catty" comes from a French word *quatre* (ka-truh). This means four. The term originally had to do with four corners.

As the phrase moved north, it changed to "kitty-corner." Today, people who live around the Great Lakes almost always say "kitty-corner."

The arrow shows where you and a friend would stand if you were catty- or kitty-corner.

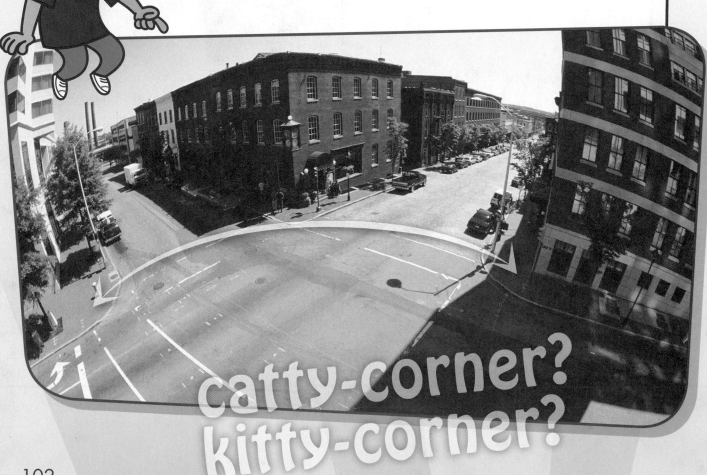

Always use a cross-walk!

catty-corner?
kitty-corner?

Regional words give us an identity. They tell about where we are from.

But Americans move a lot. Will local words ever die out? Word experts don't think so. We may pick up new words when we move. We may keep the old words. Language is always changing!

When we move, the local words we use move with us.

Hey, can you get the door?

Take the little beetle that glows in the dark. Most people in the East call it a "lightning bug." It is known as a "firefly" in the West. But just as many people use both words. As people move, they bring their dialects with them. Soon the local people mix new words with the words they used before. This is one reason that our language continues to grow and change.

Is this a lightning bug or a firefly? Many Americans use both words.

firefly? lightning bug?

I just love how it lights up!

Same Drink, Different Name

Researchers have created maps that show how words move from region to region. Foods and drinks often have the most regional names. Sometimes you can tell where someone comes from by what they call a sweet, fizzy drink. Someone from the East Coast or California will call it a "soda." People from the Midwest and Great Lakes region usually call it "pop." Southerners often call it "soft drink." What do you call it? Does your name match up with the map?

Gulp! Gulp! Gulp!

● a. soda (52.97%)
● b. pop (25.08%)
● c. soft drink (5.89%)

What Do You Think?

Why do some foods have more than one name?

Do You Speak English?

People in Great Britain speak English. So do people in the United States. But people in these two nations often use different words to talk about the same things.

For example, in England an elevator is called a *lift*. A police officer in England is called a *bobby*. People in England call a truck a *lorry*.

Atlantic Ocean

Scotland

England

Louisiana

England

United States

Great Britain is about the size of the state of Louisiana. The Atlantic Ocean separates it from the United States. A common language ties the two nations together.

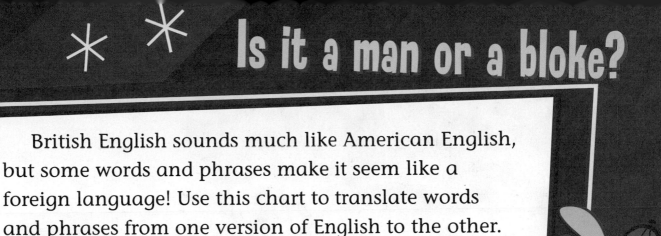

Is it a man or a bloke?

British English sounds much like American English, but some words and phrases make it seem like a foreign language! Use this chart to translate words and phrases from one version of English to the other. Try using some British English with your friends.

BRITISH ENGLISH	AMERICAN ENGLISH
bloke	man
boot	trunk of a car
bonnet	hood of a car
gobsmacked	incredibly amazed
jammy	lucky
scrummy	delicious
bite your arm off	excited to get something
afters	dessert
best bib and tucker	best clothes
pull your socks up	try to do better
chuffed	happy with something
chuck it down	rain hard
jumper	sweater
skint	have no money
cheers	good-bye
Well bowled!	Well done!

scrummy!

bobby?

COMMUNICATION

4 YOU 2 DO

Word Play

Use this week's vocabulary words to help you answer these riddles.

1. I can stand for something even though I don't have legs. What am I?

2. Tell me what you call it, and I will tell you where you are from. What am I?

Now, try writing your own riddle. Use one of this week's words or another word you know.

Making Connections

When people want to communicate, sometimes distance is an obstacle. What other obstacles get in the way when we want to communicate?

On Paper

How would your life be different without computers, television, or telephones? Write about it.

Answers for Word Play: symbol, dialect

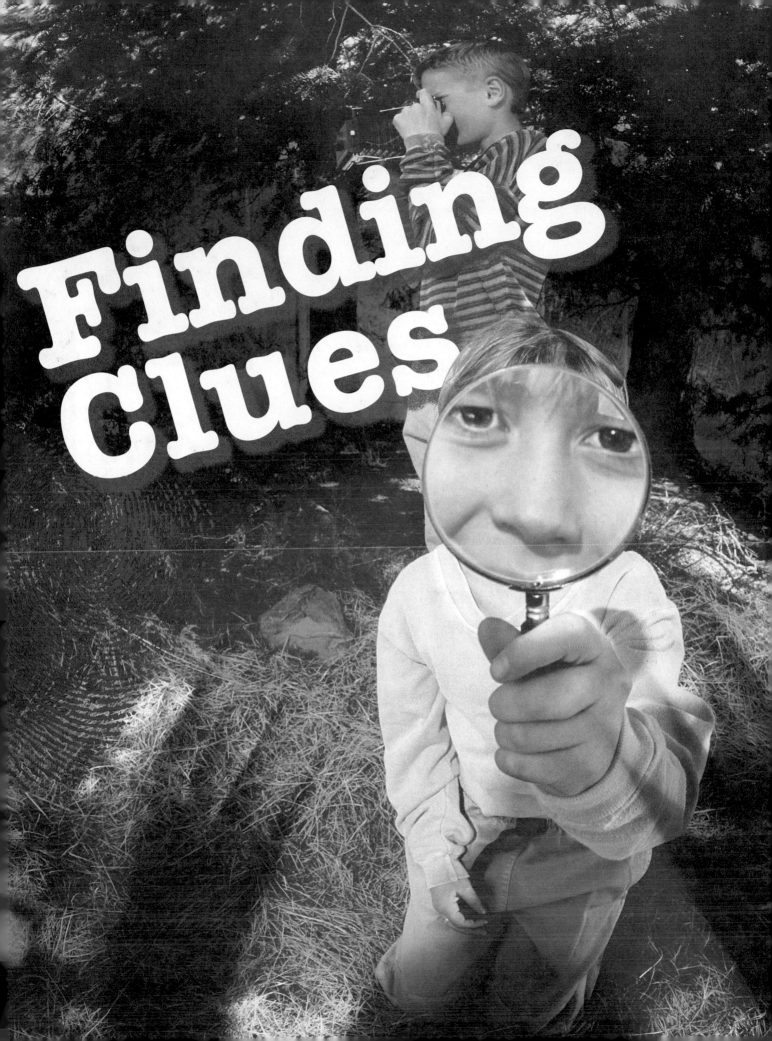

Finding Clues

Contents

Finding Clues

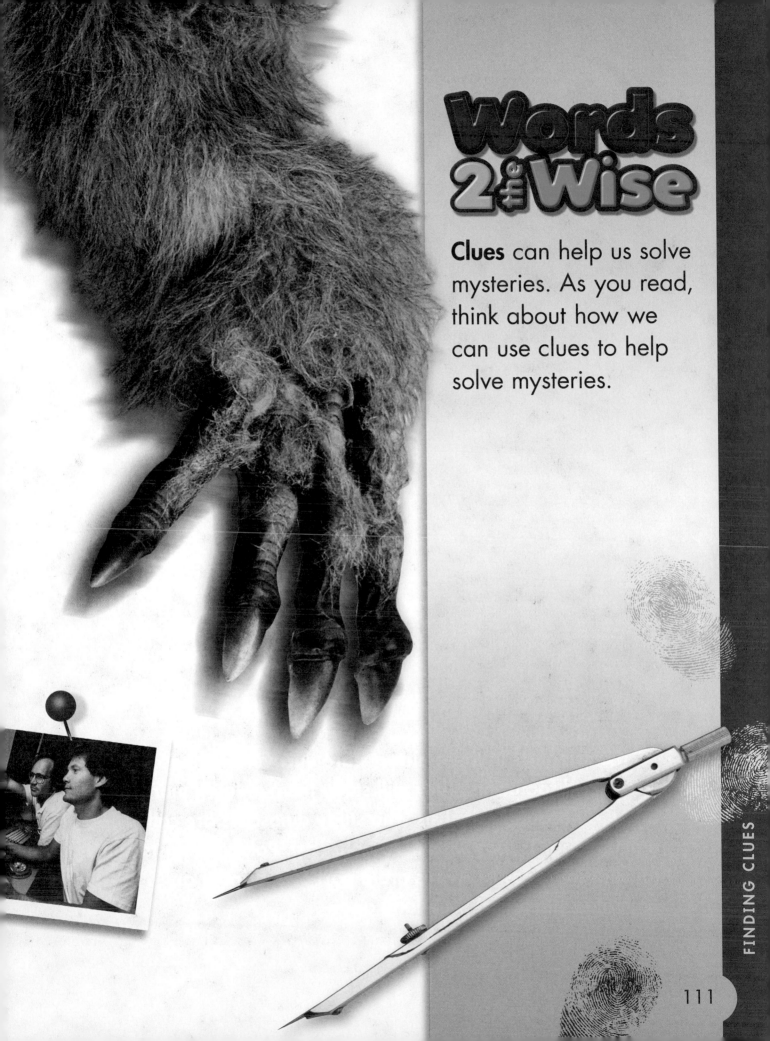

Words 2 the Wise

Clues can help us solve mysteries. As you read, think about how we can use clues to help solve mysteries.

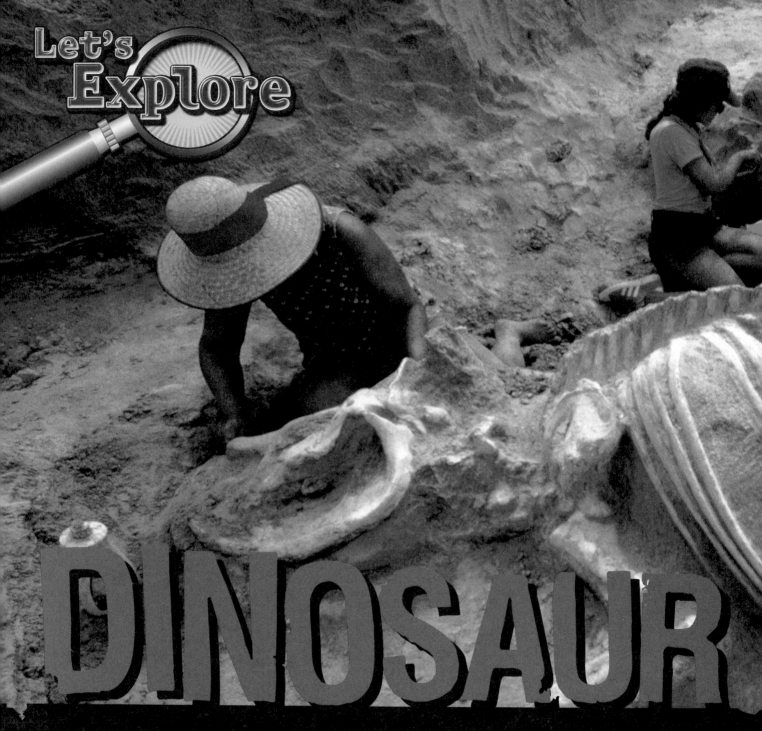

DINOSAUR

The scientists in these pictures are uncovering dinosaur bones and footprints. They will study them to learn more about dinosaurs. Scientists who study dinosaurs are called paleontologists (pay-lee-on-TOL-oh-jists). Paleontologists hunt for dinosaur fossils. Fossils are a part or a print of an animal or plant that lived long ago.

HUNTERS

They might find bones, eggs, and footprints. Fossils are not always easy to find. These scientists are skillful. They dig in sand, dirt, and stones. They look carefully to find something important. That is why these scientists are called dinosaur hunters.

THE HUNT GOES

Dinosaur hunters do more than hunt for fossils. They also study fossils to find clues about how dinosaurs lived. They look for clues about how they behaved, what they ate, and where they lived.

Paleontologists sort through thousands of bones like a giant puzzle.

ON!

They also try to solve the mystery of why dinosaurs disappeared. Dinosaur hunters have many ideas about what killed the dinosaurs. What do you think? Was it an asteroid, a volcano, an ice age, or maybe disease? No one has proof yet.

MONSTER MYSTERIES:
Bigfoot
AND Nessie

by Jennie Hissom

Bigfoot and the Loch Ness Monster are mysterious monsters. People have reported seeing these creatures for hundreds of years. But no one has ever found proof that they really exist. What do you think? Let's examine the evidence.

Big Questions About Bigfoot

Bigfoot stories have existed for centuries. Several Indian nations tell tales of these beasts. One nation calls them Sasquatch (SASS-kwatch). This means "Hairy Giant."

Stories about Bigfoot have existed for a long time. The first written mention of Bigfoot was from the year 1811. Explorer David Thompson found large footprints in the Rocky Mountains. His guide said they came from a Sasquatch.

If real, these Bigfoot tracks came from a creature about eight feet tall. It would have weighed 600 to 800 pounds.

A newspaper in Canada wrote about a mysterious ape-like creature in 1884. A train crew claimed to have captured a Bigfoot. But it escaped. The description didn't sound like a Bigfoot. It was too small. But the article helped keep the mystery alive.

The most famous clue comes from California. A man named Roger Patterson filmed a Bigfoot. He also made plaster casts of its footprints. Some experts in Hollywood saw Patterson's film. They thought the Bigfoot looked real!

Does this film show Bigfoot or someone wearing a costume?

Bigfoot Stories Live On!

1811
David Thompson sees Bigfoot footprints.

1884
Canadian newspaper reports small, Bigfoot-like creature.

| 1810 | 1830 | 1850 | 1870 | 1890 | 1910 |

Researchers from Washington State found a body print of Bigfoot in 2000. Was this just another prank?

Many people are convinced that Bigfoot is real. Willow Creek, California, even calls itself "The Capital of Bigfoot Country." One county in Washington passed a law against hunting or shooting Bigfoot!

Most scientists believe that Bigfoot footprints and pictures are fakes. This happened upon closer scrutiny. Why has no one ever captured Bigfoot? Why hasn't anyone found any Bigfoot bones?

1924
Miners' cabin attacked by group of Bigfoot creatures.

1958
Bigfoot visits construction site.

1967
Patterson films Bigfoot.

2000
Bigfoot body print found.

1930   1950   1970   1990   2010

What Lives in Loch Ness?

People in Scotland tell stories about the Loch Ness Monster. It lives in Loch Ness. Loch is the Scottish word for lake. People have nicknamed the monster Nessie. People say this mysterious creature looks like a dinosaur.

For centuries there were very few stories about Nessie. Then, in 1880, a diver named Duncan McDonald reported seeing Nessie. He was diving at the time.

As this painting shows, the Loch Ness Monster looks like no other creature on Earth.

Loch Ness Stories Live On!

1880
Diver sees Nessie.

1870   1890

A road was built along the lake in 1933. Since then more people have reported seeing Nessie.

Researchers have tried to find an explanation for the monster stories. One hunter named Sir Peter Scott even gave the monster a scientific name.

In 1972, researchers from the Academy of Applied Science tried to find Nessie too. Robert Rines used sonar and underwater cameras. Rines's sonar picked up large, moving objects. And his cameras recorded something that looked like a large flipper.

Tom Dinsdale displays a model he made of the Loch Ness Monster.

1933
Road built along Loch Ness leads to many sightings of Nessie.

1972
Rines's team finds sonar contacts and takes underwater photos at Loch Ness.

1987
Operation Deepscan searches for Nessie.

1910   1930   1950   1970   1990

In 1987, researchers used sonar to hunt for the monster. Their findings showed large, moving objects in the lake.

Scientific scrutiny showed that some of the sonar findings can be explained by underwater waves or gas. They might even be schools of fish. Still others think that there is a real creature in the lake. It could be a whale. Or it may even be a plesiosaur (PLEE-see-oh-SORE). This is a type of reptile that does not exist any longer.

Divers set up an underwater camera in hopes of taking a picture of Nessie.

Are these monsters fact or fiction? Many people think Bigfoot and the Loch Ness Monster are imaginary. They think that tales about them are legends. Or they think tales about them are pranks. Some scientists believe that they may actually exist. They claim that the photos and videos are proof. Do you think the photos are real? Watch for these monsters in the news. You may find the answer!

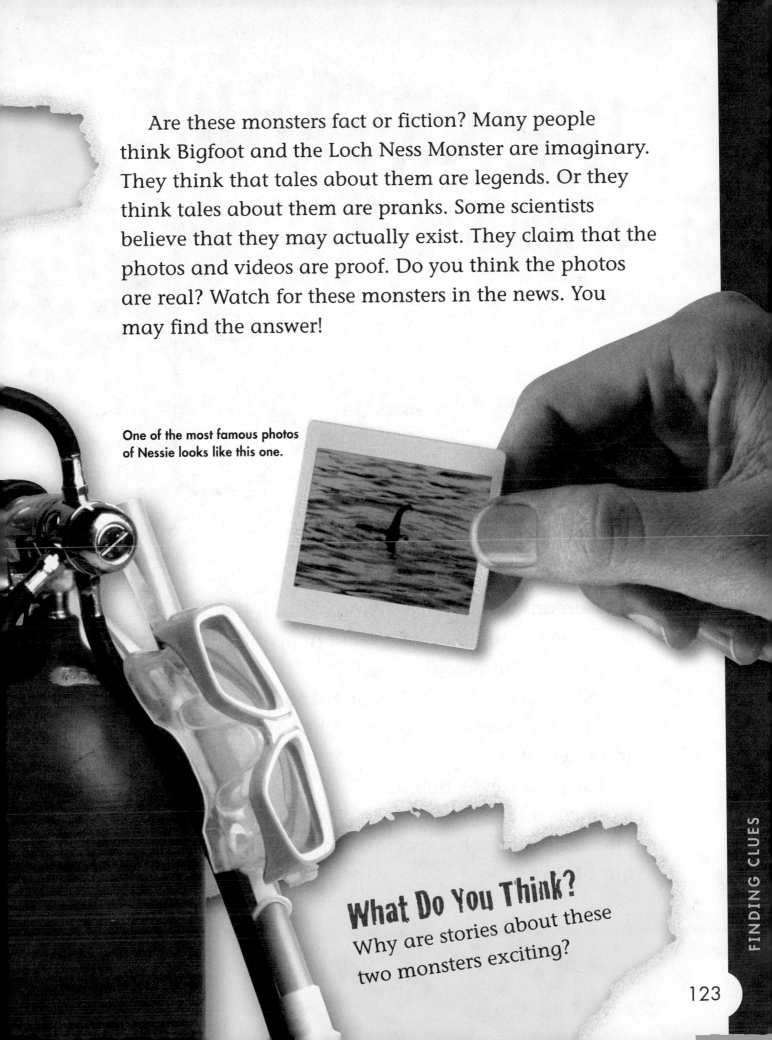

One of the most famous photos of Nessie looks like this one.

What Do You Think?
Why are stories about these two monsters exciting?

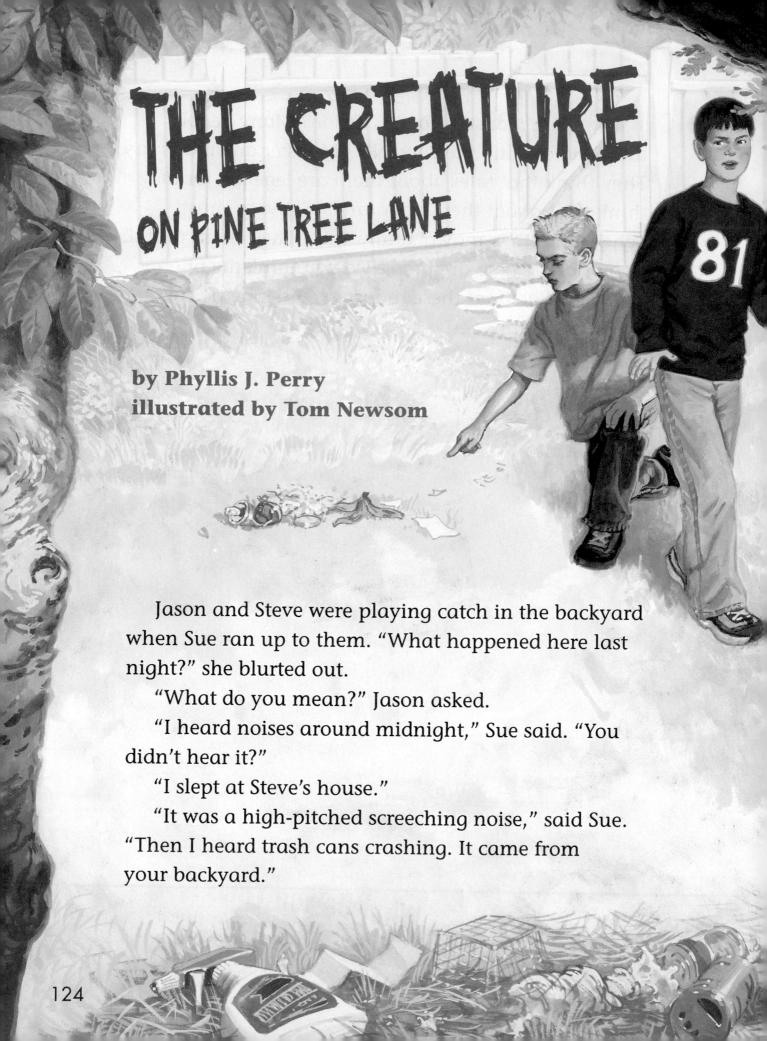

THE CREATURE
ON PINE TREE LANE

by Phyllis J. Perry
illustrated by Tom Newsom

Jason and Steve were playing catch in the backyard when Sue ran up to them. "What happened here last night?" she blurted out.

"What do you mean?" Jason asked.

"I heard noises around midnight," Sue said. "You didn't hear it?"

"I slept at Steve's house."

"It was a high-pitched screeching noise," said Sue. "Then I heard trash cans crashing. It came from your backyard."

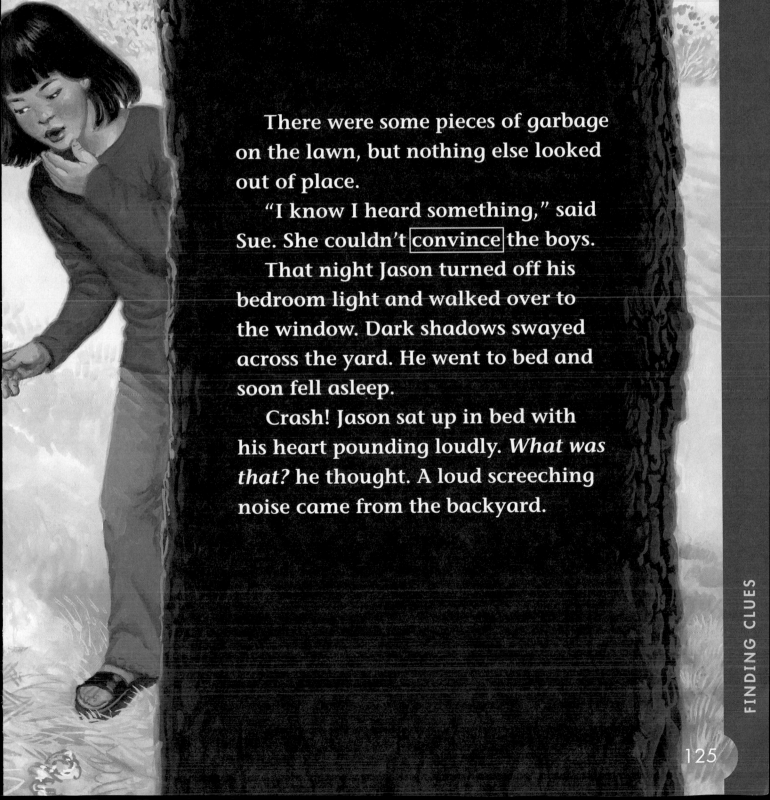

There were some pieces of garbage on the lawn, but nothing else looked out of place.

"I know I heard something," said Sue. She couldn't convince the boys.

That night Jason turned off his bedroom light and walked over to the window. Dark shadows swayed across the yard. He went to bed and soon fell asleep.

Crash! Jason sat up in bed with his heart pounding loudly. *What was that?* he thought. A loud screeching noise came from the backyard.

Jason tiptoed to the window. Scratch, scratch, scratch. Something was on the roof, right above his head. Jason poked his head out the window. He saw a large shadow passing overhead.

Jason was curious. He put on his slippers, crept downstairs, and looked into the backyard.

Something was hitting the fence. As he opened the gate it made a creaking noise. It was just a trash can knocking against the gate! He picked it up, looked around, and then went back inside.

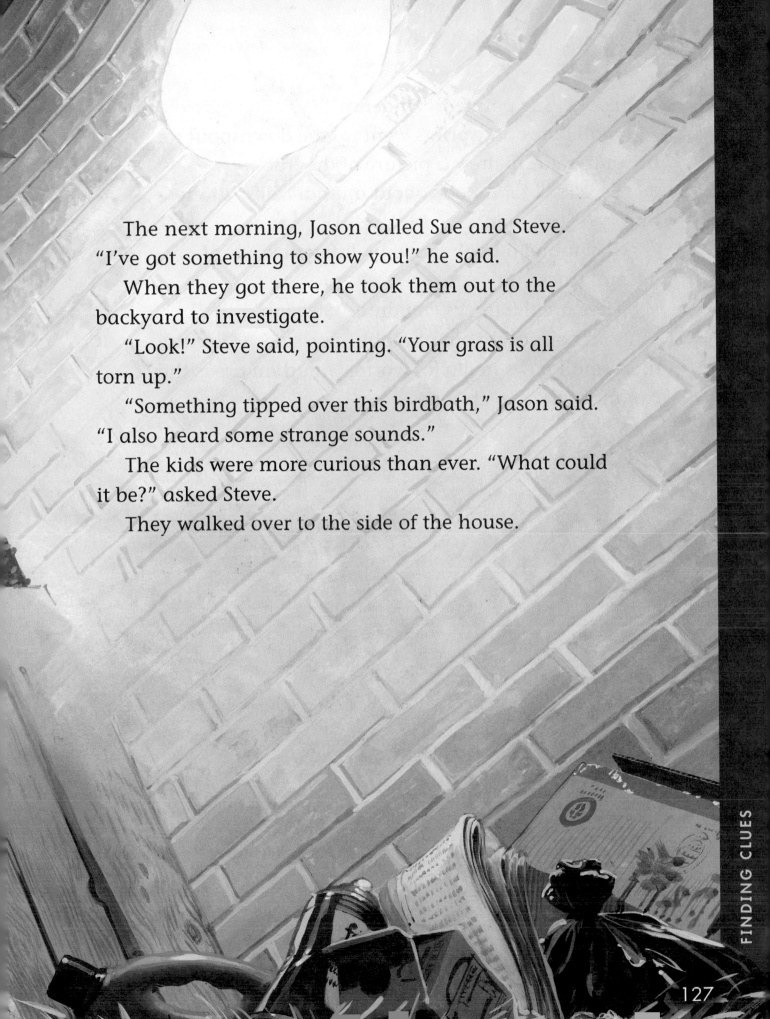

The next morning, Jason called Sue and Steve. "I've got something to show you!" he said.

When they got there, he took them out to the backyard to investigate.

"Look!" Steve said, pointing. "Your grass is all torn up."

"Something tipped over this birdbath," Jason said. "I also heard some strange sounds."

The kids were more curious than ever. "What could it be?" asked Steve.

They walked over to the side of the house.

"Look!" Sue pointed. "Evidence?"

Small black paw prints went up the downspout to the gutter. Jason drew a picture of the tracks.

"Let's look for a book about animal tracks at the library," Steve said.

They found a book showing different kinds of animal tracks.

"Here are the tracks you drew," Steve said.

"Raccoons come out at night," Sue said. "They use their small paws to dig for worms. In urban areas they can make dens in chimneys."

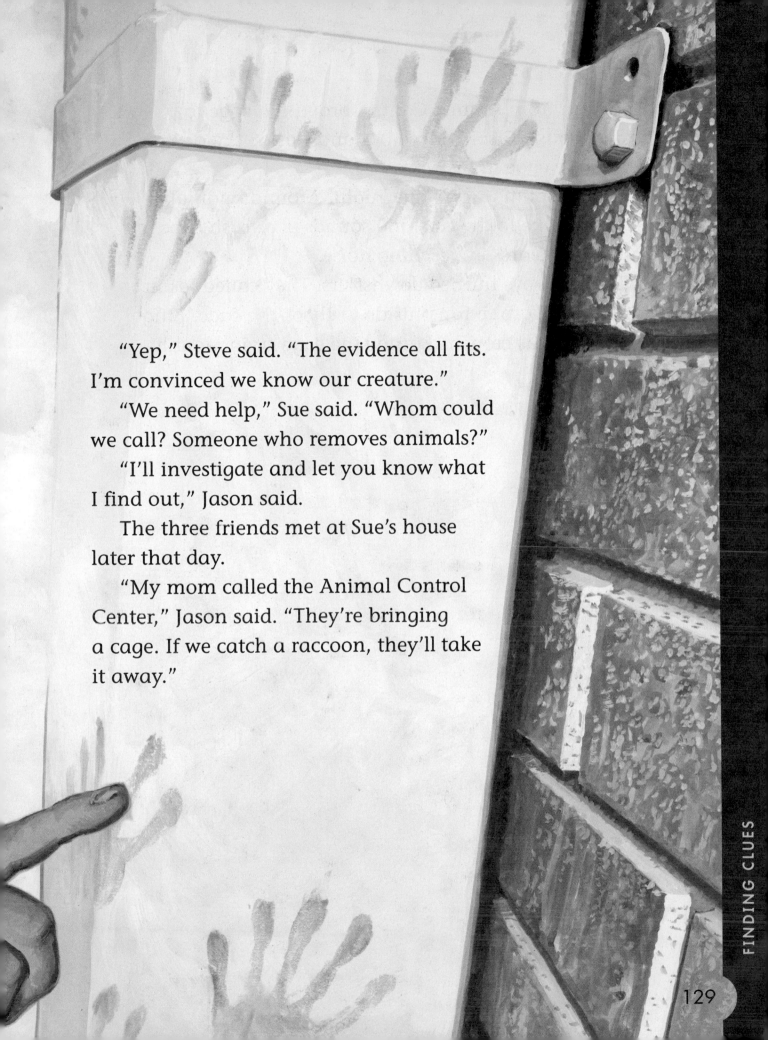

"Yep," Steve said. "The evidence all fits. I'm convinced we know our creature."

"We need help," Sue said. "Whom could we call? Someone who removes animals?"

"I'll investigate and let you know what I find out," Jason said.

The three friends met at Sue's house later that day.

"My mom called the Animal Control Center," Jason said. "They're bringing a cage. If we catch a raccoon, they'll take it away."

A man from Animal Control brought a cage to Jason's house. Jason placed bananas inside the cage. He put the cage in his backyard.

Steve slept at Jason's that night. Around midnight, the boys woke to the crashing sounds of a trash can. Then they heard a screeching noise.

The two boys hurried downstairs. They called Jason's parents. The group ran outside to check the cage. Bingo! A raccoon was crouched inside the cage crying loudly.

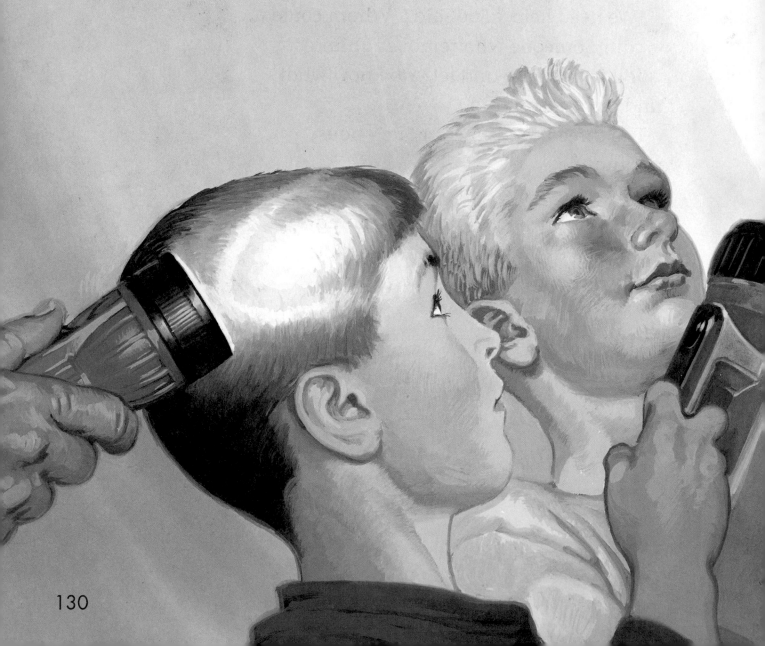

After breakfast, Jason called Sue. She came over just as the man from the Animal Control Center had come to take the raccoon away. He said he would set it free in the woods.

Jason hoped the raccoon would be happy in its new home. He knew he would be happy when all was quiet once again on Pine Tree Lane.

WHAT DO YOU THINK?

Why do you think the raccoon made a visit to Jason's backyard? What clues in the story helped you come up with your answer?

The Bermuda Triangle is the source of many strange stories.

The Bermuda Triangle is a stretch of ocean between Bermuda, Florida, and Puerto Rico. A reporter gave the area its name when he wrote an article saying that many planes and ships had disappeared there. People began to think of the Bermuda Triangle as a strange place where boats and airplanes vanish.

In 1918, a Navy ship named the USS Cyclops supposedly vanished in the Triangle. It quickly became part of the legend of the Bermuda Triangle.

ATLANTIC OCEAN

United States

Bermuda

Florida

Bermuda Triangle

Puerto Rico

Stories about the USS Cyclops claimed it went down in the Bermuda Triangle. But, the facts show it probably did not.

TRIANGLE MYSTERY

Investigators believe that the Cyclops sank during a storm in the Chesapeake Bay, hundreds of miles away from the Bermuda Triangle!

Most disappearances within the Bermuda Triangle have explanations. Some of the boats and planes that reportedly vanished in the Bermuda Triangle were not even in the Triangle! In other cases, records do show what happened, such as human error or bad weather.

The U.S. Coast Guard believes that there is nothing strange about the area. But still, the mystery remains!

Scientists study the Bermuda Triangle and track ships lost within it to solve its mystery.

4 you 2 Do

Word Play

A synonym is a word that means the same or almost the same as another word. Which of these words are synonyms?

scrutiny   evidence   examination

Hint: Two of these words are synonyms that mean "a careful look." What are some synonyms for the other vocabulary word?

Making Connections

You have read about several mysteries. Which have been solved? Which mysteries are people still collecting clues about?

On Paper

Invent your own legend about a mysterious creature or place. Include imaginary evidence!

Possible answers for Word Play: *Scrutiny* and *examination* are synonyms. Synonyms for *evidence*: proof, facts, clues

Glossary

com·bine (kəm bīn′), *VERB.* to join two or more things together: *He had to combine milk, eggs, and butter to make the cake.* **com·bines, com·bined, com·bin·ing.**

com·mu·ni·ca·tion (kə myü′ nə kā′ shən), *NOUN.* giving news or information: *Instant messaging is a form of communication.*

con·ceal (kən sēl′), *VERB.* to put or keep something out of sight; hide: *Dad concealed the surprise gift in the closet behind the coats.* **con·ceals, con·cealed, con·ceal·ing.**

con·ver·sa·tion (kon′ vər sā′ shən), *NOUN.* friendly talk between two or more people: *Their conversation went on for hours.*

con·vince (kən vins′), *VERB.* to make someone believe something: *His test score did not convince the teacher that he had studied.* **con·vinc·es, con·vinced, con·vinc·ing.**

cre·a·tive (krē ā′ tiv), *ADJECTIVE.* being able to think of new things or ideas: *She made some very creative puppets out of socks.*

cur·i·ous (kyur′ ē əs), *ADJECTIVE.* 1. eager to know something: *The little girl was very curious about how to drive a car.* 2. strange, odd, or unusual: *I found a curious old box in the garage.*

di·a·lect (dī ′ə lekt), *NOUN.* a form of language that is spoken by a group of people from the same community or area: *I could tell by his dialect that he was from Boston.*

a in hat	ō in open	sh in she
ā in age	ȯ in all	th in thin
â in care	ô in order	ŦH in then
ä in far	oi in oil	zh in measure
e in let	ou in out	ə = a in about
ē in equal	u in cup	ə = e in taken
ėr in term	u̇ in put	ə = i in pencil
i in it	ü in rule	ə = o in lemon
ī in ice	ch in child	ə = u in circus
o in hot	ng in long	

di·ver (dī′ vər), NOUN. someone who works under water wearing special equipment: *The diver found a box of gold coins on the ocean floor.*

ev·i·dence (ev′ ə dəns), NOUN. anything that shows what happened; facts: *The evidence showed that a raccoon had tipped over the garbage can.*

ex·change (eks chānj′), VERB. to give and take things of the same kind: *We exchanged test papers to check our answers.* **ex·change·es, ex·changed, ex·chang·ing.**

ex·plor·er (ek splôr′ ər), NOUN. someone who travels to unknown places to discover new things: *The explorer found pieces of pottery in the ruins.*

il·lu·sion (i lü′ zhən), NOUN. something that looks different from what it actually is: *The mirror gave him the illusion of being very tall.*

in·stinct (in′ stingkt), *NOUN.* a way of acting that an animal is born with; not learned: *Birds use instinct to fly south for the winter.*

in·ter·pret (in tėr′ prit), *VERB.* to explain the meaning of something: *She interpreted her friend's dream.* **in·ter·prets, in·ter·pret·ed, in·ter·pret·ing.**

in·ves·ti·gate (in ves′ tə gāt), *VERB.* to examine something in order to find out more about it: *The detective said he would investigate the crime scene.* **in·ves·ti·gates, in·ves·ti·gat·ed, in·ves·ti·gat·ing.**

in·vis·i·ble (in viz′ ə bəl), *ADJECTIVE.* unable to be seen: *The invisible ink could be seen only with a special marker.*

a	in hat	ō	in open	sh	in she
ā	in age	ȯ	in all	th	in thin
â	in care	ô	in order	ᵀH	in then
ä	in far	oi	in oil	ᴢh	in measure
e	in let	ou	in out	ə	=a in about
ē	in equal	u	in cup	ə	=e in taken
ėr	in term	u̇	in put	ə	=i in pencil
i	in it	ü	in rule	ə	=o in lemon
ī	in ice	ch	in child	ə	=u in circus
o	in hot	ng	in long		

ma·gi·cian (mə jish′ ən), NOUN. someone who performs tricks: *The magician pulled a rabbit out of his top hat.*

mys·ter·i·ous (mi stir′ ē əs), ADJECTIVE. hard to explain or understand: *The mysterious footprints could not be explained.*

per·cep·tion (pər sep′ shən), NOUN. understanding how something works: *She has a clear perception of how the game is played.*

phrase (frāz), NOUN. 1. a short group of words that expresses a familiar idea: *"All for one and one for all" is his favorite phrase.* 2. two or more words that have meaning but do not contain a subject and a verb: *"At school" and "in the house" are examples of phrases.*

pro·tect (prə tekt′), *VERB.* to keep someone or something safe from harm or danger; defend: *Proper food protects a person's health.* **pro·tects, pro·tect·ed, pro·tect·ing.**

re·gion (rē′ jən), *NOUN.* any place, space, or area: *Bighorn sheep live in mountainous regions.*

re·la·tion·ship (ri lā′ shən ship), *NOUN.* a connection between people, groups, and other things: *I have a good relationship with all my teachers.* *PL.* **re·la·tion·ships.**

re·sponse (ri spons′), *NOUN.* reaction by a living thing to some change in its surroundings: *When you go from a dark movie theater into bright daylight, the pupils in your eyes get smaller in response.*

scru·ti·ny (skrüt′ n ē), *NOUN.* close study or careful inspection: *No clue escaped the detective's scrutiny.*

a in hat	ō in open	sh in she
ā in age	ȯ in all	th in thin
â in care	ô in order	℡H in then
ä in far	oi in oil	zh in measure
e in let	ou in out	ə =a in about
ē in equal	u in cup	ə =e in taken
ėr in term	ù in put	ə =i in pencil
i in it	ü in rule	ə =o in lemon
ī in ice	ch in child	ə =u in circus
o in hot	ng in long	

sense (sens), *VERB.* to feel, to be aware of; to understand: *The baby rabbit could sense her mother's fear and was ready to run.* **sense·es, sensed, sens·ing.**

shout (shout), *VERB.* to call or yell loudly: *The teacher told them not to shout in the museum.* **shouts, shout·ed, shout·ing.**

sym·bol (sim′ bəl), *NOUN.* something that stands for or means the same thing as something else: *The Statue of Liberty is a symbol of freedom.* *PL.* **sym·bols.**

trans·mit (tran smit′ or tranz mit′), *VERB.* to send along; pass along: *The coach used hand signals to transmit information to the players.* **trans·mits, trans·mit·ted, trans·mit·ting.**

van·ish (van′ ish), *VERB.* to disappear suddenly: *The sun vanished behind the clouds.* **van·ish·es, van·ished, van·ish·ing.**

vis·i·ble (viz′ ə bəl), *ADJECTIVE.* able to be seen: *The shore was barely visible through the fog.*

young (yung), *NOUN.* children of humans and animals; offspring: *The mother lion cared for her young.*

a in hat	ō in open	sh in she
ā in age	ȯ in all	th in thin
â in care	ô in order	ŦH in then
ä in far	oi in oil	zh in measure
e in let	ou in out	ə =a in about
ē in equal	u in cup	ə =e in taken
ėr in term	u̇ in put	ə =i in pencil
i in it	ü in rule	ə =o in lemon
ī in ice	ch in child	ə =u in circus
o in hot	ng in long	

Acknowledgments

Illustrations

17, 98–105 Eric Larsen; **18–24** Franklin Hammond; **26–29, 106** Jim Steck; **44–50** Richard Downs; **58, 72–79** Nancy Lane; **124, 126, 130** Tom Newsom.

Photographs

Every effort has been made to secure permission and provide appropriate credit for photographic material. The publisher deeply regrets any omission and pledges to correct errors called to its attention in subsequent editions.

Unless otherwise acknowledged, all photographs are the property of Pearson Education, Inc.

Photo locators denoted as follows: Top (T), Center (C), Bottom (B), Left (L), Right (R), Background (Bkgd)

Cover (CL) ©Robert H. Creigh/Shutterstock, (CR) Jenny Risher/M Represents, Inc., (BL) Rubberball Productions; **1** (L, CL) Rubberball Productions; **2** Getty Images; **3** (B) ©Royalty-Free/Corbis, (TR) Nick Vedros & Assoc./Photographer's Choice/Getty Images; **5** (B) ©GK & Vikki Hart- Inconica/Getty Images, (TR) ©GK Hart/Vikki Hart,The Image Bank/Getty Images, (T) ©Scott Morgan/Taxi/Getty Images, (Bkgd) Getty Images; **6** (CR) Library of Congress; **7** (BR) ©Royalty-Free/Corbis, (BR) Comstock Inc., (TC) Getty Images, (C) Rubberball Productions; **8** (C) ©Ralph Crane//Time Life Pictures/Getty Images, (CL, BR) ©Rick Davis/Darkride & Funhouse Enthusiasts; **9** (TL) ©Rick Davis/Darkride & Funhouse Enthusiasts, (BR) ©Rubberball Productions; **10** (L) Library of Congress; **11** (TR) Comstock Inc., (TR, T) Library of Congress; **12** (C) ©Bettmann/Corbis, (BR) Corbis; **13** (TL) Creatas, (TR) The Granger Collection, NY; **14** (C) ©Harry Price/Mary Evans Picture Library; **15** (TR) Getty Images, (BR) Library of Congress; **16** (T) Bettmann/Corbis, (BR) The Granger Collection, NY; **17** (BL) ©Royalty-Free/Corbis; **30** (R) Rubberball Productions; **31** (C) Paul A. Souders/Corbis; **32** (C) ©Royalty-Free/Corbis, (CR) ©Juniors Bildarchiv GmbH/Alamy; **33** (L) Getty Images; **34** (C) ©Harry Engels/Photo Researchers, Inc., (CL) ©Roger Leo/PhotoLibrary Group, Inc.; **35** (C) ©Royalty-Free/Corbis, (T, BR, BL) Getty Images; **36** (C) ©Frans Lanting/Corbis, (TR) Getty Images; **37** (R) Getty Images; **38** (R) Frank Siteman/Index Stock Imagery; **39** (TR) Getty Images, (L) Joe McDonald/Corbis; **40** (T) ©Juniors Bildarchiv GmbH/Alamy; **41** (R) Martin Harvey; Gallo Images/Corbis; **42** (Bkgrd) ©Joe Ausin Photography/Alamy Images, (TR) Jupiter Images; **43** (B) Getty Images; **56** (R, CL) Getty Images; **57** (C) ©Nicholas Rigg/Getty Images; **58** (TR) ©Joe Robbins/Getty Images; **59** (TR) ©James Nielsen/AFP/Getty Images, (CL) ©Nathan Blaney/Getty Images; **60** (C) ©Corbis/SuperStock, (TL) ©Paul Spinelli/MLB Photos/Getty Images; **61** (R) ©James Nielsen/AFP/Getty Images, (L) ©Joe Robbins/Getty Images; **62** (T) ©G Fiume/Getty Images, (TL) Getty Images, (BL) Jupiter Images, (B) Thomas Coex ©AFP/Getty Images; **63** (CR) ©John Holden/Getty Images, (C) Noah Graham/©NBAE/Getty Images; **64** (BR) ©Jason Stitt/Shutterstock; **66** (TR) ©Tomasz Trojanowski/Shutterstock; **67** (BR) ©Erik Isakson/Getty Images; **68** (BL) ©Randy Faris/Corbis; **69** (BR) ©John-Francis Bourke/Corbis; **71** (T) ©Robert H. Creigh/Shutterstock; **80** (C) ©Roman Sigaev/Shutterstock, (BR) Alinari Archives/Corbis, (TR) Library of Congress; **82** (BR) ©Nathan Blaney/Getty Images; **83** (L) ©Tom Stewart/zefa/Corbis, (TL, TC, CR, BC) Getty Images, (TR) Image Source/Getty Images; **84** (CR) Getty Images, (BR) Stockdisc, (TR) T. Kevin Smyth/Stock Connection; **85** (T) ©Creatas, (B) BananaStock, (CL) Jack Delano/Library of Congress; **86** (C) ©George H. H. Huey/Corbis; **87** (C) T. Kevin Smyth/Stock Connection; **88** (CL) John Giustina/Getty Images, (C) Pete Turner/Getty Images; **89** (C) Matthias Kulka/Corbis; **90** (CR, BR) Getty Images; **91** (CR) ©Hot Ideas/Index Open, (TL) ©Walden Fawcett, Washington, D.C./Library of Congress; **92** (TR) ©Royalty-Free/Corbis, (CL, BR, BL) Getty Images, (CR) Jack Delano/Library of Congress; **93** (CR, BL, BC) Getty Images; **94** (C) ©Jerry Cooke/Corbis, (CL, BR, BL) Getty Images; **95** (BL) ©Hot Ideas/Index Open, (TR) ©Science Museum/Science & Society Picture Library, (TL) Adam Bartos, Time & Life Pictures/Getty Images; **96** (TR, CR, BR, BL) Getty Images, (CL) Image Source/Getty Images; **97** (BR, BL) Getty Images; **98** (R) Comstock Images; **99** (C) Jade Lee/Getty Images, (BR) Stockdisc; **100** (BR) White Cross Productions/Getty Images; **101** (CR, BL) Getty Images; **102** (B) Getty Images; **103** (C) BananaStock, (BL) Getty Images; **104** (BR) ©Creatas, (BL) Richard T. Nowitz /Alamy Images; **108** (R) BananaStock; **109** (CL, C) ©Royalty-Free/Corbis; **110** (TC) ©The Natural History Museum, London/Alamy Images, (CR, BR) Getty Images; **111** (BL) Acey Harper, Time & Life Pictures/Getty Images, (BR) Getty Images, (C) Jenny Risher/M Represents, Inc.; **112** (C) ©Annie Griffiths Belt/Corbis; **113** ©Arctic Images/Alamy Images, (CR) ©The Natural History Museum, London/Alamy Images; **114** ©Marc Hill/Alamy Images, (BR) Pascal Goetgheluck/Photo Researchers, Inc.; **115** (BR) Richard T. Nowitz/Photo Researchers, Inc.; **116** (L) First Light /ImageState; **117** (C) Bettmann/Corbis, (B) Jenny Risher/M Represents, Inc.; **118** (C) Fortean Picture Library, (CL) Getty Images; **119** (BR) First Light /ImageState, (TR) Getty Images; **120** (L) Gino D'Achille/Bridgeman Art Library; **121** (C) Bettmann/Corbis, (BL) Getty Images; **122** (B) Emory Kristof/Getty Images; **123** (CR, BL) Getty Images, (C) Keystone/Getty Images; **132** (CL) Bettmann/Corbis, (BC) Corbis, (TR, C) Getty Images; **133** (BC) Acey Harper, Time & Life Pictures/Getty Images, (BL) Getty Images; **134** (TL) ©Royalty-Free/Corbis, (R) Jenny Risher/M Represents, Inc.; **136** (C) Blend Images/Getty Images; **138** (C) Getty Images; **140** (TR) Blend Images/Getty Images; **142** (CR) Getty Images; **143** (B) Getty Images.